DO JOB-SPECIFIC PROBLEMS AND INDIVIDUAL PROBLEM-SOLVING ABILITIES MEDIATE THE RELATIONSHIPS BETWEEN PERSONALITY AND CAREER COMMITMENT? AN EMPIRICAL INVESTIGATION.

A Dissertation

Presented to the Faculty of the College of Business Administration of Trident University International

in Partial Fulfillment of the Requirements for the Degree of Doctor of Philosophy in Business Administration

by

Crystal Michelle Washington Cypress, California

2017

Defended February 17, 2017

Approved by:
Office of Academic Affairs
Date of Degree Conferral: April 9, 2017
Dean: Dr. Debra Louis
Director, Ph. D. Program: Dr. Indira Guzman
Committee Chair: Dr. Roger Rensvold
Committee Member: Dr. Joshua Shackman
Committee Member: Dr. Giorgio Canarella

ProQuest Number: 10264941

All rights reserved

INFORMATION TO ALL USERS
The quality of this reproduction is dependent upon the quality of the
copy submitted.

In the unlikely event that the author did not send a complete manuscript
and there are missing pages, these will be noted. Also, if material had
to be removed, a note will indicate the deletion.

ProQuest 10264941
Published by ProQuest LLC (2017). Copyright of the Dissertation is
held by the Author.

All rights reserved.
This work is protected against unauthorized copying under Title 17,
United States Code Microform Edition © ProQuest LLC.

ProQuest LLC.
789 East Eisenhower Parkway
P.O. Box 1346
Ann Arbor, MI 48106 - 1346

© 2017 Crystal M. Washington

DO JOB-SPECIFIC PROBLEMS AND INDIVIDUAL PROBLEM-SOLVING ABILITIES MEDIATE THE RELATIONSHIPS BETWEEN PERSONALITY AND CAREER COMMITMENT? AN EMPIRICAL INVESTIGATION.

Crystal M. Washington, Ph.D.

Trident University International 2017

Previous research has explained career commitment (CC) in terms of personality differences (e.g., conscientiousness, unfriendliness, and neuroticism; Aluja & Garcia, 2004), as well as behavioral consequences (e.g., promotion, recognition, verbal warnings, or removing privileges; Podsakoff, Bommer, Podsakoff, & MacKenzie, 2006). No study has specifically examined the relationship between personality and CC from an interactional perspective; specifically, as the interaction between the individual differences that define personality, and individual perceptions of the job environment. The purpose of this study was to establish a causal link between personality traits and CC, in the context of the types of problems that characterize work in a specific career. This quantitative, cross-sectional study examined the theoretical links between personality and CC by assessing the mediating and moderating relationships between specific thinking abilities, perceptions of the problem environment, and career self-efficacy (CSE). As part of this study, a new scale for quantifying the perception of the problem environment was developed and found to have significant reliability based on responses to the survey to the pilot study. This new scale, the Perception of the Problem

Environment Scale (PoPES) is the study's main theoretical contribution, inasmuch as the perception of the problem environment, considered as either a main effect or a moderator, may be an important factor in predicting behaviors other than CC. The Partial Least Squared Structural Equation Modeling (PLS-SEM) was used to test theoretical link between personality traits and CC, in the context of problem solving abilities. Results indicated that Conscientiousness was significantly associated with higher levels of convergent thinking ability. CSE was significantly predicted by higher levels of divergent thinking ability. CC was significantly predicted by CSE. Other significant and relevant findings and practical implications are discussed. This project increased the understanding of CC, by incorporating the effects of a previously unexamined environmental factor the perceived problem environment. This study contributed to the study of an unfamiliar phenomenon, the perception of the problem environment, and future researchers may attempt replication of this instrument to increase confidence in its use to enhance the future of the organizational behavior field of study.

KEYWORDS: convergent thinking, divergent thinking, problem solving, big five personality traits, career commitment, career self-efficacy, perception of the problem environment

BIOGRAPHICAL SKETCH

Ms. Crystal Washington possesses over 23 years of leadership and experience in human resources management, project management, acquisition, information technology and contracting in the military, private, and federal business sectors. Prior to assuming her current position with the US Department of Agriculture Food Safety & Inspection Services (USDA- FSIS) as Chief, Program Management Branch, Program Management Division, Office of the Chief Information Officer, Crystal served as a Senior Program Analyst/Project Lead on the Marine Corps Enterprise Information Technology Services Technology Refresh Design and Build effort supporting the Marine Corps Systems Command. She previously served as a Senior Acquisition Analyst/Associate in the private sector where she conducted contract policy, research, and development, as well as, assisted in the development of an automated information system portal. As a US Army Officer, she performed as an Adjutant General Officer (Human Resources), Acquisition/Project Manager, and a Contingency Contracting Officer. Crystal served honorably in the United States Army, retiring as a Major.

Prior to pursuing her Doctor of Philosophy degree in Business Administration with a concentration in Management and Organizations, Crystal earned her Bachelor of Business Administration (BBA) from Savannah State University and a Master of Arts in Human Resources

Development from Webster University. She is Federal Acquisition Level III Certified as a Contracting Officer Representative and in Program/Project Management.

DEDICATION & ACKNOWLEDGEMENT

First, I would like to thank God; I was never left nor forsaken on this journey. Second, this dissertation is dedicated to my two nieces, Laila and Lauryn Polk. Their smiling faces, determination in school, encouragement, and prayers gave me a newfound appreciation for their significance in my life. Many thanks to Dr. Roger Rensvold for being unrelentingly intense at times and emotionally intelligent enough to strike the right balance to effectively encourage me through the end of this process. Dr. Rensvold made this one of the most important and formative experiences I have ever had in my life.

To the members of my dissertation committee, Dr. Indira Guzman, Dr. Joshua Shackman, and Dr. Giorgio Canarella, I am sincerely appreciative of your support. You all have generously given of your time and expertise to help me better my work, and I am eternally grateful for that.

I am grateful to many people who shared their respective experiences in this same pursuit, especially Mr. Chauncey Cowell, Dr. Peter Mangles, Dr. Ashley Leigman, Dr. Roderick French, and Dr. Cernata Morse. Each of them gave me the courage to challenge myself to contribute to the field of organizational behavior and to never give up on this endeavor.

I must acknowledge my best friend and sister, Mrs. Yvette Polk, family members, several dear friends and colleagues who constantly helped me keep perspective on what is most important in life. I am more than indebted to my wonderful parents, Ronald and Eva Williams, whose knowledge, wisdom, support and love knows no bounds. Throughout my life, my parent's motto was always to "keep on keeping on", and those words helped me continue to put one foot in front of the other down the home stretch to see my hard work yield one of my greatest accomplishments.

Table of Contents

BIOGRAPHICAL SKETCH v
DEDICATION & ACKNOWLEDGEMENT vii
CHAPTER 1: INTRODUCTION 1
    Personality and CC 1
    Problem Statement 2
    Purpose and Rationale of the Study 3
    Gaps in the Literature that Justify the Present Study 6
    Overview 9
    Research Questions 10
    Primary RQ: 11
    The Variables 12
    Summary and Preview 14
CHAPTER 2: LITERATURE REVIEW 16
    Introduction 16
    Section 1: Personality Traits and Behavior 17
    Personality 17
    Traits and Behavior 18
    Evolution and Development of the Five
    Factor Model (FFM) 19
    Big Five Theory 20
    Implications for Managerial Work 21
    Section 2: Thinking Abilities 28
    Personality and Thinking Abilities 29
    Section 3: Perception of the Problem Solving Environment 30
    Section 4: Overview of Theories and the Construct Model
    Concerning Personality and Career Commitment 32
    Section 5: Hypotheses Concerning Personality
    Traits and Thinking Abilities 36
    H1a: Openness to Experience and
    Divergent Thinking Ability 37
    H1b: Conscientiousness and Convergent
    Thinking Ability 38

H2a: Divergent Thinking and CSE 38
H2b: Convergent Thinking and CSE 39
H3a and H3b: Perception of the Problem Environment (open vs. closed) Moderates the Relationships between Thinking Abilities (Convergent vs. Divergent) and CSE 40
Extraversion, Agreeableness, and Neuroticism 42
H4: CSE and CC 42
Summary 43
Hypotheses 45

CHAPTER 3: RESEARCH METHODOLOGY 46
Introduction 46
Research Design 47
Study Population and Power 48
Data Collection Tools & Procedures 51
Variables and Measurement Instruments 55
Measurement Quality Assessment 55
Measurement of Personality 58
Measurement of Thinking Abilities 59
Measurement of the Perception of the Problem Environment 60
Measurement of CSE 64
Measurement of Career Commitment 65
Measurement of Demographic & Control Variables 65
Statistical Analysis 67
Limitations 69
Correlation and Causation 69
Internal Validity 70
External Validity 71
Potential Bias 71
Confidentiality and Ethical Assurance 73

CHAPTER 4: DATA ANALYSIS AND RESULTS 74
Introduction 74
Pilot Study 75
Primary Study, Data Cleaning & Screening 78
Descriptive Statistics 78
Assumptions Testing 80

    Model Specification and Quality Assessment 80

    Post Hoc PoPES Analysis 81

    Internal Reliability and Validity Analysis 83

    Structural Equation Model 85

    Hypothesis Testing Results 85

    Summary 93

Chapter 5: DISCUSSION, IMPLICATIONS & CONCLUSION 94

    Discussion, Implications, and Conclusion 94

    Results and Outcome Summary 95

    H1a: Openness to Experience is positively
    correlated with Divergent Thinking Ability. 95

    H1b: Conscientiousness is positively
    correlated with Convergent Thinking Ability 96

    H2a: Divergent thinking ability is positively
    correlated with CSE 96

    H2b: Convergent thinking is positively
    correlated with CSE. 97

    H3: An open problem environment negatively moderates the
    association between divergent thinking ability and CSE and
    H3b: A closed problem environment will positively moderate the
    association between convergent thinking ability and CSE 97

    H4: CSE is positively correlated with CC. 98

    Implications to Theory 98

    Practical Implications of the Research 100

    Limitations of the Research &
    Recommendations for Future Direction 102

    Conclusion 103

    APPENDIX A (Pilot Study Consent Form):
    CONSENT TO PARTICIPATE IN RESEARCH 106

    CONSENT TO PARTICIPATE IN RESEARCH 106

    PURPOSE OF THE STUDY 106

    PROCEDURES 106

    CONFIDENTIALITY 107

    POTENTIAL RISKS AND DISCOMFORTS 107

    POTENTIAL BENEFITS TO SUBJECTS
    AND/OR TO SOCIETY 107

    PAYMENT FOR PARTICIPATION 108

    PARTICIPATION AND WITHDRAWAL 108

IDENTIFICATION OF INVESTIGATORS	108
RIGHTS OF RESEARCH SUBJECTS	109
SIGNATURE OF RESEARCH SUBJECT OR LEGAL REPRESENTATIVE	109
PROPOSED PERCEPTION of the PROBLEM ENVIRONMENT SCALE (PoPES)	111
(Modified) GENERALIZED SELF-EFFICACY SCALE	112
APPENDIX A (Primary Study Consent Form) CONSENT TO PARTICIPATE IN RESEARCH	115
CONSENT TO PARTICIPATE IN RESEARCH	115
PURPOSE OF THE STUDY	115
PROCEDURES	115
CONFIDENTIALITY	116
POTENTIAL RISKS AND DISCOMFORTS	116
POTENTIAL BENEFITS TO SUBJECTS AND/OR TO SOCIETY	116
PAYMENT FOR PARTICIPATION	117
PARTICIPATION AND WITHDRAWAL	117
IDENTIFICATION OF INVESTIGATORS	117
RIGHTS OF RESEARCH SUBJECTS	118
SIGNATURE OF RESEARCH SUBJECT OR LEGAL REPRESENTATIVE	118
APPENDIX B: BIG FIVE INSTRUMENT (BFI)	121
APPENDIX C: REMOTE ASSOCATION TEST (RAT)	122
APPENDIX D: ALTERNATE USES TEST (AUT)	123
APPENDIX E: PERCEPTION of the PROBLEM ENVIRONMENT SCALE (PoPES)	125
SCORING INSTRUCTIONS	127
APPENDIX F: (Modified) GENERALIZED SELF-EFFICACY SCALE	128
APPENDIX G: CAREER COMMITMENT MEASURE (CCM)	130
Psychometrics:	132
APPENDIX H: DEMOGRAPHIC QUESTIONNAIRE	133
APPENDIX I: IRB APPROVAL LETTER	135
GLOSSARY	136
BIBLIOGRAPHY	137

CHAPTER 1

INTRODUCTION

Personality and CC

The long-term commitment people bring to their work lives is important for companies to remain globally competitive, as well as, ensuring sustainable growth (Ho & Yeung, 2015).

However, valuable experience walks out the door whenever somebody quits a job for a change of career, and the losing organization incurs expenses for recruitment and training. The Bureau of Labor Statistics (2015) noted that the turnover rate of individuals in private and government sectors were close to 3 million. In addition, replacing employees is estimated to cost employers on average $30,000 a year for low-paying jobs and $213,000 a year for high-paying jobs (Merhar, 2013). Because of its practical importance, employee turnover (and its converse, CC) have received extensive attention from several perspectives. According to one perspective, known as Trait theory, a person's tendency to either stay with or change a career is the result of stable individual differences. On the other hand, the Theory of Reasoned Action (TRA) posits a more complex mechanism; a person's behavior, to include career change, is dependent upon attitudes towards the behavior and reasoned judgements about its consequences. This proposed research will combine the two.

Problem Statement

Previous research has explained CC in terms of personality differences (e.g., conscientiousness, unfriendliness, and neuroticism; Aluja & Garcia, 2004), as well as behavioral consequences (e.g., promotion, recognition, verbal warnings, or removing privileges; Podsakoff, Bommer, Podsakoff, & MacKenzie, 2006). No study has empirically investigated the interactional perspective views of personality and CC, behavior as the product of individuals, with individual differences, responding to their job- specific perceptions of the environment.

The purpose of this quantitative, cross-sectional, study will be to examine the theoretical links between personality and CC by assessing the mediating and moderating relationships between specific thinking abilities, perceptions of the problem environment, and CSE. As part of this proposed study, a new scale for quantifying the perception of the problem environment has been developed. This new scale, the Perception of the Problem Environment Scale (PoPES), will be the study's main theoretical contribution, inasmuch as the perception of the problem environment, considered as either a main effect or a moderator, may be an important factor in predicting behaviors other than CC. This project will increase the understanding of CC, by incorporating the effects of a previously unexamined environmental factor; the perceived problem environment. Its practical application will lie in an enhanced ability to match people with careers.

Both personality and CC, have been studied extensively; accordingly, the unique perspective this study brings to the relationship between them will be carefully explained. But in the first instance, we will discuss these two constructs in considerable detail

Purpose and Rationale of the Study

The overall purpose of this study is to conduct a cross-sectional survey of diverse people in a myriad of professions in order to explore the relationships between their personality traits and their levels of CC as predicted by their thinking abilities, moderated by their perceived problem solving environment, and mediated by their CSE. Further, the proposed study may be used as a self-assessment tool by the participants to better understand their view of open and closed problems and to determine their commitment to a particular career. It may afford managers an opportunity to understand the fit or lack of fit between their thinking abilities and perceptions of their problem-solving environments. The proposed study advances the organizational behavior field of study by using personality traits as it applies to CC. The study breaks down the broad and multi-dimensional aspects of both variables, and it identifies personality traits as a particular manifestation of an individual's intent to commit to a career. The primary outcome of this study will be a predictive model that may be useful in career counseling and personnel selection.

This study has several practical purposes as well. When preventing turnover, employers should be more concerned about CC, as opposed to organizational or affective commitment, because CC is the best predictor of whether or not an employee will remain in their current position. Mrayyan and Al-Faouri (2008) conducted a study on nurses to examine their CC and motivation. Their study found that CC was the best and most significant predictor of the nurse's CC and influenced their job performance.

Career commitment is slowly developed and cultivated over time. With organizations less able to guarantee employees job satisfaction, CC is becoming a competitively strategic advantage to human resources selection and retention of personnel (Rashid and Zhao, 2010). CC is a construct that is commonly used in the literature, including the construction of statistical models (e.g., Kumar & Bakhashi, 2010; Mrayyan & Al-Faouri, 2008, Poon, 2004; Riveros & Tsai, 2011). CC is a broad multidimensional concept, defined as "the strength of one's motivation to work in a chosen career role" underpinned by the Career Motivation Theory (London, 1983). Its concepts include (a) individual needs, interests, and personality variables potentially relevant to one's career, incorporating domains of career identity, career insight, and career resilience); (b) situational or work related environment factors that influence career motivation, such as staffing policies and procedures, leadership style, job design, group cohesiveness, career development programs, and the compensation system; and (c) extra factors related to the demands of one's work and family.

Occupational Commitment is a unidimensional concept that is also extensively used in the literature, including the construction of statistical models (e.g., Irving, Coleman, & Cooper, 1997; Kim & Mueller, 2010; Simola, 2011). It refers specifically to an individual's affective reaction to his or her occupation, exemplified by the definition given by Goswani, Mathew & Chadha, N.K. (2007) as follows: "Occupational commitment is the psychological link between an individual and his occupation that is based on an affective reaction to that occupation. Thus a person with higher occupational commitment strongly identifies and has positive feelings towards his occupation" (p. 13).

This study will not merely measure affective reactions (e.g., whether or not an individual is emotionally attached to, and whether or not s/he likes the job); but also several other occupation-related variables, including specific thinking abilities, perceptions of the career environment, and CSE, which are not necessarily related to affective reactions. This implies that the correct dependent variable is CC rather than Occupational Commitment. "Career" is a more general construct than "occupation," inasmuch as a career may consist of several occupations, pursued either concurrently or consecutively.

The study considers the multi-dimensional aspects of both variables, personality and commitment, and it identifies personality traits that are predictive of an individual's intent to commit to a career. The proposed study advances the field of organizational behavior by applying personality traits to the study of CC. In addition to the theoretical contributions, the proposed study will also provide employees with a self-assessment tool to better understand their view of open and closed problems, which can be used to determine their commitment to a particular career. For managers, this study will afford them an opportunity to understand the fit or lack of fit between their employees' thinking abilities and perceptions of problem-solving environments to deter a lack of CC.

Gaps in the Literature that Justify the Present Study

This study will fill gaps in the literature and add to the existing body of management knowledge by making three unique contributions. First, this proposed study will examine how specific personality dimensions are related to workplace behavior, as moderated by the perception of the problem environment. This is in accordance with Barrick, Mount, and Judge's (2001) called for a moratorium on further meta-analytic studies that naively examined how the Big Five personality dimensions were linked to performance. As an alternative, they encouraged researchers to develop new agendas and explore new directions. Several Big Five and CC studies (Andi, 2012; Judge, Heller, & Mount, 2002; Judge, Higgins, Thorescn, & Barrick, 1999; Grady, 1989) have examined predictors such as emotional intelligence, innovation, turnover, absenteeism, job satisfaction, and job performance; however, these variables were examined as first-order predictors, not as mediators or moderators, and the dependent variable was performance rather than commitment. This study will be the first to explore a model linking personality traits with CC, in the context of problem solving abilities.

Second, no past research has established a theoretical link between personality traits and CC, in the context of the types of problems that characterize work in that career (Blau, 1985; Blau, 1988; Hackney, 2012). Consequently, jobs, and indeed career fields, are characterized by the types of problems that need to be solved on a day-to-day basis. In this study, the types of problems typically encountered will be referred to as the problem environment. As explained below, this study characterizes the environment as either open or closed, depending upon whether the problems are themselves open or closed. One example of a closed environment, characterized by problems having well-defined sets of relevant factors and strong rules for solving them, is a police department. An example of an open environment would be a medical clinic specializing in the treatment of rare contagious diseases. The doctors working there would encounter cases that are poorly understood, and have few guidelines concerning either diagnosis or treatment. It seems that the problem environment is a fundamental characteristic of an organization.

To date, however, no instrument has been devised to measure a person's perception of the problem environment. The word perception is critical here as two people in the same environment may view it quite differently. If the researcher were attempting to categorize the perception of the problem environment in some absolute sense, then that would be a problem; but since the researcher is attempting to predict individual behavior, it is not. It is a person's perceptions that matter; indeed, some people, such as deep salvage divers, thrive in environments that others would find terrifying. In response to the lack of an instrument, the researcher is developing one called the Perception of Problem Environment Scale (PoPES) (Appendix E).

The development of the PoPES is the crux of the theoretical contribution to the proposed study and organizational behavior. A pilot study is a crucial element to the design of my study because it increases the likelihood of a successful study and improves the internal validity of the survey questions and research process. The instrument will be piloted to test its validity and reliability; after which, it will be refined and administered as part of the primary study.

Third, this study will also be the first to uniquely determine methodologically if higher levels of conscientiousness and openness to experience increase or decrease CSE, moderated by the perceived characteristics of the perception of the problem environment. The gaps in the literature provide a rationale and direction for the proposed study. For instance, Blau (1988) examined the construct and measurement of CC using participants from both a newspaper and insurance companies. He also recommended a future direction of CC research to explore "the causes of career commitment" (p. 295). This study follows that recommendation.

Overview

In this short introductory section, an overview of a conceptual model is presented (Figure 1). The variables are outlined in this chapter. Specific hypotheses are developed in Chapter 2; the details of variable operationalization, instrumentation and analysis are also deferred to Chapter 2.

The first premise of the research is that personality bears some relationship to CC. CC is a type of decision; a decision to remain in a particular occupation, however that may be defined. As a decision, it can be analyzed in terms of Fishbein and Ajzen's (1975) TRA which posits, in part, that the decision to do something is affected by the perceived likelihood of doing it successfully.

The perceived probability of success is closely related to perceived ability, also known as CSE. Accordingly, this study posits that CSE, another well-studied construct, mediates the relationship between thinking abilities and CC.

Given the centrality of problems and problem-solving in managerial work, I am most concerned with individual problem-solving abilities, and the types of problems that need to be solved. The remaining problem-related constructs complete the model and are discussed in detail in the following sections.

Personality is related to two distinctly different ways of thinking; convergent thinking, and divergent thinking. The problem environment, as perceived by the problem-solver, is characterized by the types of problems requiring solution. The problem types fall on a continuum ranging from *open* to *closed*.

The motivation to conduct this study lies within the model. Reading the complete model (Figure 1) from left to right: Personality is correlated with different ways of thinking. These interact with the perceived environment to produce an assessment of CSE which, in turn, is correlated with CC. This model exhibits the theoretical link between personality and CC.

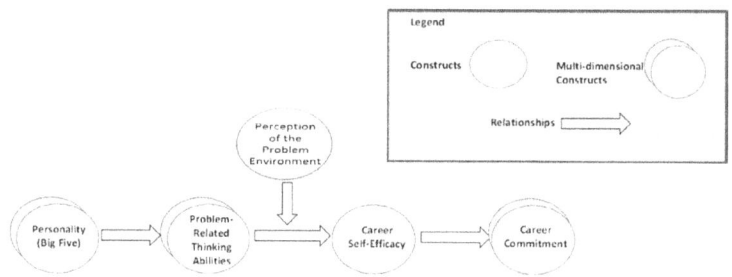

Figure 1. Conceptual model: Personality & Career Commitment

The hypotheses concerning relationships between the variables are developed in Chapter 2. The variables introduced below are discussed in detail in Chapter 2. But at this point, it is appropriate to introduce the primary research question, together with four ancillary questions.

Research Questions

No study has yet examined how job-specific problems and individual problem-solving abilities mediate the relationship between personality and CC. I propose each research question to determine whether job-specific problems and an individual's problem-solving abilities mediate the relationship between personality and CC. This study aims to build on prior literature by further testing the theoretical relationships between personality traits and CC as defined as thinking ability, perception of the problem environment, and CSE. Since there is no practical approach to examine personality and the perception of the problem environment as two independent variables to predict CC; there has to be a causal chain of other variables, and the exploration of distal (personality; trait dimensions) and proximal (problem-solving) attributes will determine if these have an impact on an individual's CC. The multi-dimensionality of this concept predicts an individual's behaviors toward organizational outcomes and knowledge of this can provide managers with a tool to improve individual employee's commitment to their career.

Primary RQ:

Do job-specific problems and individual problem-solving abilities mediate the relationship between personality and CC?

Ancillary RQs:

1. How does personality, in conjunction with the problem environment that characterizes a career, affect a person's commitment to that career?
2. How is personality correlated with specific thinking abilities?
3. How does a person's perception of the career environment interact with their problem-solving abilities, to produce an estimate of CC?
4. How is CSE related to CC?

The Variables

Constructs are complex psychological concepts (e.g., personality traits) that cannot be measured directly; however, they can be inferred by compositing indicators of their multiple facets, using statistical methods such as factor analysis (Gorsuch, 1983). In consideration of the information provided, Table 1 summarizes the constructs that will be operationalized into quantitative variables in this study.

The dependent variable is CC. The principle independent variable is personality, and its effect on problem-solving ability. The principle moderator, which is also the most original part of the study, is the perceived problem environment. The fundamental idea motivating the study is people whose problem-solving abilities favor their career environments are more likely to display high levels of CC. The varying complexities of each variable will be discussed in detail in Chapter 2.

Table 1

Conceptual Definitions of Variables

Variable	Conceptual Definition
Agreeableness	A personality trait with characteristics ranging from compassion to antagonism (Huey & Weisz, 1997, p. 405). Agreeableness is characterized as being trusting, conforming, sympathetic, and cooperative (John & Srivastava, 1999, as cited in Barlett & Anderson, 2012, p. 870).
Conscientiousness	A personality trait characterized by careful planning, organization, self-discipline, attention to detail and hard-work (Wiggins, 1996). Similarly, Kumar & Bakhshi (2010) espoused that conscientiousness denotes self-discipline and implies individual's hard work, emotional attachment, and connection to a task or an organization.

Extraversion	A personality trait characterized by an individual's outwardly directed emotions (Huey & Weisz, 1997). Extraversion is characterized by a "tendency to be self-confident, dominant, active, and excitement seeking" (Bakker, Van der Zee, Lewig, & Dollard, 2002, p. 4).
Neuroticism	A personality trait defined as having persistent levels of poor adjustments to stress, anxiety, and depression (Huey & Weisz, 1997). Neuroticism is characterized by emotional instability, anxiety, and aggression (Bartlett & Anderson, 2012).
Openness to Experience	A personality trait characterized by receptiveness to new experience, being imaginative, and independent (Wiggins, 1996). Openness to experience is characterized by curiosity, creativeness, and insightfulness (Bligh, Kohles, & Pillai, 2011).
Convergent Thinking Ability	A thinking ability involving the evaluation of several alternative solutions to find a single correct solution, or one that has the highest probability of being effective (Guilford, 1967). Convergent thinking is most effective in situations where an answer already exists and needs to be recalled or worked out. The use of existing data in a singular and logical manner is characteristic of convergent thinking (Gomez-Mejia, Balkin, and Cardy, 2007).
Divergent Thinking Ability	A thinking ability characterized by the fluidity and originality of new ideas and may be linked to the solving of open problems, to generate alternative solutions (Guilford, 1967). Divergent thinking typically develops as a spontaneous, free-flowing process, where a host of creative ideas and possibilities are generated (Gomez-Mejia et al., 2007).
Open Problem	An open problem does not have an obvious boundary. It is usually unfamiliar and often has several solutions. It requires reasoning that tends to go beyond the rules of logic. It has unpredictable outcomes that are dependent upon uncertain external influences, and the deadlines for solution are generally flexible (Mele, Pels, & Polese, 2010).

Closed Problem	A closed problem has an obvious boundary. It is usually familiar and generally has only one solution. It is solved using logical rules of reasoning. The outcomes are predictable (not influenced by uncertainty), and the deadline for a solution is generally prescribed (Mele, Pels, & Polese, 2010).
Perception of the Problem Environment	Applying the notion of "open" versus "closed," mentioned above, problems are classified along a continuum, ranging from closed to open. Each individual perceives his or her problem-solving environment in a different way, based upon the prevalence of either open or closed problems (Christakos & SpringerLink (Online Services, 2011).
Career Self-Efficacy	An individual's beliefs in their ability to perform a task or successfully accomplish work-related matters (Feehan & Johnston, 1999). It can be defined as people's judgments of their abilities to perform career behaviors in relation to career development, choice, and adjustment (Anderson & Betz, 2001; Niles & Sowa, 1992).
Career Commitment	A behavioral intention which means that if an individual is attached to a job and organization, and likes what they do in that position, then the individual is more likely to present a high level of CC (Goulet & Singh, 2002).

Summary and Preview

This proposed quantitative study, based on a cross-sectional survey, will focus on the construction and evaluation of a statistical model linking personality traits to CC. The predictive model is underpinned by a theoretical framework, based on the TRA, the Big Five Factor Model of personality traits, and Career Motivation Theory. Chapter 2 describes and justifies the choice of the variables and instruments used in this study. It also provides the empirical and theoretical framework based on the literature that drives the research questions and hypotheses. Chapter 3 presents the rationale for the methodology based on the purpose and objectives outlined in Chapter 1. Additionally, Chapter 3 provides a more detailed description of the population, sampling procedure, and the data collection and analytical procedures.

CHAPTER 2

LITERATURE REVIEW

Introduction

In this project, I propose a model linking personality traits with CC, in the context of the types of problems that characterize that career. The practical value of the model, if it is validated, will be to predict which people, as characterized by specific personality traits, are more or less likely to be committed to particular careers (characterized by the types of problems that the practitioners typically encounter). The causal links in the model will be presented as testable hypotheses, and evidence supporting those hypotheses will be presented. The figure presented in Chapter 1 depicted the proposed model at the conceptual level. In this chapter, detail is added to ensure Figure 2 depicts the model at a level where it can be tested at the construct level.

This chapter has five sections. In the first section, I provide a general discussion of personality traits and their associations with behavior. The first two sections focus on the association between personality traits, behaviors, and thinking styles. The third section defines the characteristics of a problem solving environment. The fourth section develops hypotheses relating personality traits with thinking abilities. The fifth section develops hypotheses about the associations among CC and CSE.

Section 1: Personality Traits and Behavior

Research surrounding personality as a construct predictive of behavior took a hiatus during the 1980s because investigators focused on single instances of behavior, and viewed constructs that evolved over time, such as attitudes and behaviors, to be unstable. However, research on personality began to reemerge once aggregated, longitudinal data about personality and situational variability became available. As a result, our understanding of personality as an antecedent of behavior increased substantially.

The subsections of this section focus on the following topics:

- Personality
- Traits and Behavior
- Evolution and Development of the Five Factor Model
- Big Five Theory
- Implications of Personality for Managerial Work

Personality

Personality is one of the main constructs of this study. The personality construct is difficult to operationalize because it is influenced by many internal and external factors, processes, and has many facets. There are many theories of personality, none of which satisfies all personality theorists.

Traits are components of personality. They are the broad dimensions of an individual's personality. They are integral to defining an individual's uniqueness, and to predicting his or her unique behavior, to include the acquisition and processing of information (Chamorro-Premuzic & Reichenbacher, 2008). Everybody has traits, and personality is generally viewed as a stable combination of traits that determine behavior. It is self-defining, and adaptive to differences in culture, social class, and other conditions (McAdams & Pals, 2006).

Traits and Behavior

In the early 1900s, the concept of traits was just emerging. At that time, less clearly defined terms, such as temperament, characteristics, and personality were being used, and used interchangeably; however, they are distinct (Cloninger, Svrakic, & Przybeck, 1993). In Cloninger et al.'s 1993 work, he defined temperament as a basic inherited style used to regulate individual moods and tendencies; whereas, character refers to an individual's adaptation and adjustment to his or her environment.

Traits refer to distinctive patterns of behavior, or individual characteristics that have implications for behavior and behavioral outcomes (Matthews, Deary, & Whiteman, 2003). Traits are relatively immutable. Traits are continuous and prominent aspects of behavior. Traits can explain how individuals perceive an environment, the beliefs they bring to that perception, their affective responses to it, and how they react to it. According to Allport (1961), traits may be classified as cardinal (dominant and shaping an individual's behavior, such as orientations towards money or fame), central (basic components of personality; such as honesty, intelligence, creativity), and secondary (an individual's disposition toward things, in specific situations).

The corpus of research findings and theories concerning traits is known, not surprisingly, as Trait Theory. The theory is incomplete, and rife with controversy. Some theorists assert that traits are strongly predictive of discrete behaviors. Others argue that traits are more foretelling of patterns, rather than of specific instances, of behavior. Still others argue that while traits may be correlated with behaviors, they do not explain them; that is, they do not elucidate the causative mechanisms that are the proximate causes of the behaviors. Trait Theory is useful as an organizing principle; it provides lists. Its usefulness is limited by ambiguity about what should go under the headings on the lists. In general, Trait Theory does not account for situational moderators and mediators of behavior; nor does it provide much guidance about leadership efficacy and workplace outcomes. In its small way, this study will attempt to provide some insight into these topics.

Evolution and Development of the Five Factor Model (FFM)

Beginning in the 1970s, researchers proposed many different traits and dimensions of personality. Early work by Tupes and Christal (1992) identified four major traits:

agreeableness, dependability, emotional stability, and culture. Later work went further in this direction, providing more definition and clarity.

The upshot of numerous factor-analytic studies was the Five Factor Model (FFM). This model reduced the number of salient traits to five, known as the Big Five (De Fruyt, McCrae, Szirmak, & Nagy, 2004; Gurven, von Rueden, Massenkoff, Kaplan, & Vie, 2013; McCrae & John, 1992; McCrae & Costa, 2008; O'Connor, 2002; Tupes & Christal, 1992). Although some controversy continues about nomenclature, Costa and McCrae (1992) demonstrated the general validity of the structure. The Big Five, those traits defined by the FFM, have been intensively researched using a variety of instruments, testing theories about their effects on behavior, the predictability of behavior, and the implications of that behavior for individuals, their leaders, and their work performance.

Big Five Theory

The FFM has been studied extensively by investigators in many different disciplines.

The Big Five traits which comprise the theory are listed in Chapter 1, Table 1, along with short definitions. From the factor-analytic point of view, the Big Five personality traits are essentially orthogonal, meaning that they are conceptually uncorrelated (Costa & McCrae, 1985; Goldberg, 1993). Nevertheless, empirical studies have identified significant multicollinearity (i.e., inter-correlations) among them (Digman, 1997). The magnitude and structure of these correlations are inconsistent, and the reasons underlying the correlations remain unclear. Researchers using exploratory factor analysis have proposed that the correlations arise because the Big Five do not represent the most rudimentary dimensions. If this is true, even broader personality traits may exist at higher levels, defined by fewer factors, each of which incorporates inter-correlated elements of the Big Five (DeYoung, 2006, Musek, 2007; Anusic et al., 2009).

Implications for Managerial Work

The Big Five, although universal, have specific implications for managers in organizations. Researchers and practitioners continue to explore traits as predictors of employees' similarities, differences, job suitability, behaviors, and affective responses to situations, job performance, and CC.

Models relating personality traits to job performance have been proposed but are still tentative; the associations seem to be more complex and nuanced than expected. The inconsistencies in current research findings prompted Barrick, Mount and Judge (2001) to call for "a moratorium on further meta-analytic studies" (p. 9) that attempt to link the Big Five to performance; instead proposing new directions, such as the associations between the Big Five and other workplace outcomes. This study will consider possible implications of the Big Five for managerial performance.

Conscientiousness. Of the Big Five, conscientiousness is consistently found to be one of the most prominent (Judge, Klinger, Simon & Yang, 2008). Tett (1998) conducted a study reviewing the association between conscientiousness and job performance. Subject to cautions and caveats, he found that conscientiousness, although a strong predictor of job performance for managers in more structured, rule-bound, conservative jobs, may impede managers whose jobs may require them to be more investigative, critical, and creative in how they manage situations, personnel, and other resources.

Tett (1998) argued that there may be maladaptive reasons whereby conscientiousness hinders job performance and may adversely impact an individual's approach to situations and their decision quality. Indeed, several studies indicate that excessively high levels of conscientiousness are associated with decrements in job performance (Le, Oh, Robbins, Ilies,

Holland & Westrick, 2011; LaHuis, Martin & Avis, 2005). Specific shortcomings that are often found in employees with very high levels of conscientiousness include excessive attention to small details at the expense of larger project goals (Tett, 1998), as well as excessive rigidity in problem solving and lack of openness to alternative solutions (LePine, Colquitt, & Erez, 2000; Martocchio & Judge, 1997).

Perhaps the most well-articulated theoretical model of the inhibitory effects of conscientiousness on performance has been proposed by Le et al. (2011). They suggested that the job performance of highly conscientious employees can be adversely affected by difficulties in problem solving. They suggest highly conscientious employees often have difficulties with solving problems that require flexibility and creativity due to excessive rigidity in problem definition, and lack of openness to alternative solutions (Mount, Oh, & Burns, 2008; Tett, 1998). They suggest that overly conscientious employees may be less willing to acquire new skills and information, or enlist new resources to solve problems (LePine, Colquitt, & Erez, 2000; Martocchio & Judge, 1997). Excessively conscientious employees may define success as the perfectionistic implementation of a specific approach to solving a problem, while losing sight of whether the solution that the employee is pursuing adequately addresses the wider goal or problem facing the organization.

 More recent investigations, based on Le et al.'s (2011) initial work, linked excessive levels of conscientiousness to the decision-making performance of management executives. In a broad review of current research on personality and managerial performance, Pierce and Aguinis (2013) examined the notion that personality traits that have positive effects at moderate to high levels may have deleterious effects when they are present at extremely high levels. Pierce and Aguinis (2013) label this association the "Too much of a good thing (TMGT)" effect. In particular, the notion that, in some contexts, extremely high levels of conscientiousness may have deleterious effects on managerial problem solving may help to explain some puzzling findings in the literature concerning personality traits and managerial performance. In spite of the fact that many reviewers have claimed that conscientiousness is a nearly universal predictor of job performance across all occupations, including management positions (Barrick et al., 2001), Pierce and Aguinis (2013) suggest that more recent meta-analysis of research on conscientiousness and performance is not as consistent as previously claimed. Pierce and Aguinis (2013) suggest that moderate and extreme levels of conscientiousness may represent different traits with regard to managerial behavior; the latter may reflect pathological rigidity and inflexibility, rather than adaptive levels of concern for quality and detail.

Openness to experience (Openness). This construct refers to "individuals whose behavior tends to be creative, imaginative, and curious to experience new things amongst other things" (Klang, 2012; Costa & McCrae, 1992). Openness to experience was found to be related to creativity as well as the ability to adapt to change (Barrick & Mount, 2005; George & Zhou, 2001; LePine, Colquitt& Erez, 2000). Specifically, individuals with a high level of openness to experience have been described as being imaginative, artistic, cultured, curious, original, broad- minded, and intelligent (Klein & Lee, 2006). These types of individuals are highly motivated, seeking new and diverse experiences and preferring to become engaged in unfamiliar situations. Similarly, individuals who are said to have a low level of openness to experience are said to be more conservative and tend to prefer familiar, conventional ideas (Costa & McCrae, 1992).

Specifically, it is noted that individuals who are curious, original, and independent tend to be better at dealing with change and are more likely to contribute to greater innovation at work. However, Klang (2012) found no association between job performance and openness to experience, and also points out that previous research is not in agreement with respect to the association, if any, between openness to experience and job performance.

Similarly, Judge et al. (2008) defined openness to experience as a trait that characterizes people who prefer novel, diverse, and unconventional experiences. As with conscientiousness, there are inconsistencies in the extant literature about its predictability of job performance given its dimensionality, the moderating effects of situation, and the trait's differential impact on various occupational groups (Griffin & Hesketh, 2004). Consistent with the above, several studies have noted that individuals who exhibit high levels of this personality trait tend to be creative artistic, visionary, and original. According to Judge et al. (2008), high levels of openness to experience result in the individual being against authority, rules and guidelines, as well as "difficulties working in hierarchical or traditional work settings" (p. 337). Similarly, to conscientiousness, openness to experience is not always found to be a good predictor of performance. Griffin and Hesketh (2004) used a meta-analysis to investigate openness to experience and job performance, and found it to be a poor predictor of job performance; if the work environment does not support creativity, the person may develop low intrinsic motivation and pursue non-work activities that allow for more creativity. In summary, Griffin and Hesketh (2004) characterized openness to experience as one of "the most controversial, least understood, and least researched of the five factors" (p. 243).

The remaining three of the Big Five: extraversion, agreeableness and neuroticism will be discussed briefly below. These dimensions have more to do with interpersonal relations, and therefore, affect how well problem solutions are implemented. However, they have less to do with how to arrive at solutions. These have been shown to be related to workplace performance, but only in specific cases (Barrick & Mount, 2005; Barrick et al., 2001). Arguably, this is because the three traits are more closely related to associations between the individual and others; therefore, they may be more salient to the social aspects of performing a task, rather than to the characteristics of the task itself.

Extraversion. Extraversion is defined as the "quantity and intensity of energy directed outwards into the social world" (Wechsung, 2014, p. 126). Research has found extraversion to be associated with job performance in jobs which involve a significant level of interaction with others, especially when this involves influencing others, and obtaining status and power. In these types of positions, being sociable and assertive is considered a positive trait which will likely contribute to success (Barrick & Mount, 2005). Extraversion was associated with "getting ahead," and was considered a "niche trait" (Hogan & Holland, 2003). Klang (2012) also found Extraversion to have a positive, moderate correlation with job performance. Balthazard, Potter, and Warren (2002) conducted a study on extraversion and its effect on virtual teams and their interaction. In a virtual, rather than a face-to-face situation, the investigators were unable to find "a significant relationship between extraversion and (the team goal of) solution acceptance" (p. 9).

Agreeableness. Agreeableness refers to a characteristic of "individuals who tend to be trusting, helpful toward others, forgiving, soft hearted, and compassionate" (Wechsung, 2014, p. 126). Agreeableness significantly predicted performance in positions that require substantial interpersonal interaction. In addition, agreeableness was determined to be important in cases where the interaction involved helping, cooperating, and nurturing others (Barrick & Mount, 2005). Agreeableness has been found to be particularly important in situations where working as part of a team is an important component of the work. In these cases, individuals who are low in agreeableness tend to be less effective at teamwork, and are also more likely to engage in behaviors that are counterproductive (Barrick & Mount, 2005). Previous research found agreeableness to be a "niche trait" (Hogan & Holland, 2003), which refers to its narrow range of relevance. Supporting that judgment, the research conducted by Klang (2012) found no association between agreeableness and job performance, a result also observed by Barrick and Mount (1991). Stilson (2005) examined archival data that assessed the association between agreeableness and team performance. He found that rapid decision making, due to a lack of discord and facilitated by high levels of agreeableness, has a negative effect on problem solving and decision making in groups.

Neuroticism. Neuroticism is described as being shy, angry, insecure, depressed, vulnerable, and anxious (Klang, 2012; Costa & McCrae, 1992). Specifically, neuroticism has also been defined as being antithetical to emotional stability, with a moderate negative correlation with job performance (Klang, 2012). Persson (2009) examined interaction effects between effortful control (one's ability to prevent a dominant response to perform a subdominant response) and neuroticism in a sample of 64 individuals; they found a "negative relation with active (engaging) coping styles, such as problem solving" (p. 4).

In sum, conscientiousness and openness to experience seem to be related to the association between the person and the nature of the task, while the other traits seem to be related to interpersonal relationships that may moderate the association between the person and the task. I suspect the moderating effect is complex and varies greatly across job contexts; and for that reason, extraversion, agreeableness and neuroticism are not central to this study.

Section 2: Thinking Abilities

In general, thinking abilities are not easily learned or taught. They are relevant to management practice because of their effect on an individual's ability to find workable solutions to problems. The application of thinking abilities does not depend upon the knowledge facts, formulas or algorithms, and the person's ability to use that knowledge, but rather on the ability to develop strategies to solve a problem (Carson, 2007). Lee (2004) argues that a strong ability to find workable solutions contributes to high levels of job performance. Consequently, organizations need to ensure that their employees have the right mix of thinking abilities in order to achieve the highest levels of performance.

With regard to problem solving, Guilford (1983) identified two types of thinking, which he described as convergent and divergent. These guide a person's approach to exploring, analyzing, and solving problems. Convergent and divergent thinking ability are parts of Guildford's larger framework of intellect. This consists of three different categories of thinking abilities: cognitions, product, and evaluation. Convergent and divergent thinking belong to the product category.

Convergent and divergent thinking are not mutually exclusive, but rather endpoints of a continuum. A mixture of the two may be applied to solving a problem. For example, the results of divergent thinking, consisting of several problem solutions based upon a host of ideas and possibilities, may be organized and structured by convergent thinking. This combination of abilities, working together, ideally results in the identification of a single optimal solution or correct answer from among multiple alternatives (Cropley, 2006).

Personality and Thinking Abilities

Arguably, there are links between personality traits and thinking abilities. McCrae (1987) argued that openness to experience underlies divergent thinking because the former provides raw material, in the form of facts and ideas that support the creative syntheses of the latter. Several empirical studies have suggested that individuals who exhibit high levels o openness to experience are more capable of dealing with diverse viewpoints, and of generating novel ideas that span disparate fields. King, Walker, and Broyles (1996) proposed that openness to experience is the broadest of the five personality dimensions. As a correlate of creativity, it allows for the transformation and adaptation of concepts in ways that facilitate problem solving. Several researchers found that most, if not all, individuals utilize both convergent and divergent thinking (Ashton-James, Maddox, Galinsky & Chartrand, 2009) and shift from one to the other in response to situational requirements, and that this shifting is largely independent of personality traits (Ashton-James et al., 2009; Le et al., 2011).

Section 3: Perception of the Problem Solving Environment

Problem solving refers to the process of applying knowledge and innovative ideas effectively, in order to identify, analyze, and frame solutions to problematic issues and challenges (Carson, 2007). The process is strongly affected by the problem solving environment, which is a collection of relevant requirements, issues, resources, constraints and other factors.

Problem solving is not an exclusive responsibility of those occupying the executive suite. Many organizations seek to strengthen their position and competitive advantage, by cultivating problem-solving skills in their workforce. Every individual needs to be prepared and equipped to meet the problem-solving challenge (Marone & Blauth, 2004). Although considerable research has examined individual problem-solving ability, less research has been conducted on problem-solving environments, and their interactions with abilities (Bodea & Buchman, 2012). **General Systems Theory**

In Chapter 1, I characterized the structure of a problem-solving environment by borrowing a concept from General Systems Theory (GST); namely, the concept of "open" versus "closed." A system consists of elements which are in exchange and circumscribed by a boundary which is defined by an individual. Elements can be virtually anything; exchanges are the relationships that exist between the elements; and the boundary is anything that separates the system from the environment.

The GST perspective considers a system as a set of interacting elements that acquires inputs from the environment, processes them, and possibly releases them back to the environment (Crane, 2003). The General System Theory differentiates between closed and open systems. Figuratively speaking, a closed system has an impervious boundary – a wall – around it. It is independent of the environment. Closed systems are hard to find in social and organizational science; one example from natural science would be the inside of a star. Another, less exact example would be the interior of a Dewar flask, but that is only closed until somebody opens it. On the other hand, an open system has only a notional boundary -- a chalk line, so to speak --around it. The system is defined by the person wielding the chalk. An open system is influenced by (1) its internal elements, (2) elements in the environment, and (3) elements that straddle the line between the environment and the system. An example of an open system is an organizational culture, which comprises a diverse collection of values, symbols, rituals, stories, heroes, and villains that encompass all the perceptions and assumptions held by the members of an organization. Organizational culture is an open ended system that influences people in many different ways because it is created by complex interactions with others and operates outside of people's awareness, so it has no sharply defined boundaries (Ravasi & Shultz, 2006). This study applies this notion of the open vs. closed system to classifying types of problems.

Most problems, however, cannot be clearly pigeonholed into either the "open" or the "closed" category. Open and closed problems are not mutually exclusive, but are extremes of a continuum. A problem may initially be considered to be open, because it appears to have several solutions, which emerge as a consequence of divergent thinking. These solutions may subsequently be considered to be parts of a closed problem that can be structured into a single solution by convergent thinking (Cropley, 2006). Furthermore, the processes involved in problem solving may differ across expertise and knowledge domains. For example, physical scientists are generally able to agree upon one solution to a problem – e.g., the neutron cross- section of a U238 atom -- whereas "social science problems seldom have solutions about which experts are in complete agreement. An effect of such lack of agreement is that the solver must provide arguments supporting why the proposed solution should be adopted" (Voss, Greene, Post, & Penner, 2004, p. 169).

Section 4: Overview of Theories and the Construct Model Concerning Personality and Career Commitment

In Chapter 1, a general overview of the variables and the conceptual model are explained, and in subsequent sections of this chapter, I discuss the specific parts of the model, to include the history and structure of each variable and the theoretical justifications for each of the hypotheses. This chapter provides a comprehensive overview of the intrinsic relationship between the underpinning theories, specific variables, and hypotheses outlined and depicted in the proposed construct model in this study. The specific variables mentioned in Chapter 1 were derived from principles and concepts underpinned by the TRA, the Big Five Factor Model of personality traits, the General Systems Theory, and the Career Motivation Theory.

The TRA provides the main theoretical framework for this study. It was selected for this study because of its supporting evidence of an individual's behavioral intent. The theory acknowledges the subjectivity of norms and their influence on attitudes and behaviors that motivate an individual's approach to do things and behave the way that they do (Ajzen 1988; Fishbein & Ajzen 1975; Werner 2004). Further, the TRA (Ajzen & Fishbein, 1975; Fishbein & Ajzen, 1980) posits that an individual's behavioral intention (i.e., the extent to which an individual takes action with respect to a specific situation in a particular environment) is dependent upon the individual's attitudes toward the behavior (including his or her perceptions about the consequences of performing the behavior). If an individual has a strong behavioral intention to take action, because the individual's attitudes toward that behavior are positive, then it is likely that the individual will do it. On the contrary, if an individual has a weak behavioral intention to take action, because the individual's attitudes towards that behavior are negative, then it is likely that the individual will not do it. The TRA has been tested empirically in numerous studies across many behavioral intentions such as healthy eating, consuming genetically engineered foods, and limiting exposure to the sun (Ajzen, Albarracin, & Homik, 2007). The behavioral intention that I propose to study is CC, which means that if an individual is attached to a job and organization, and likes what s/he does in that position, then the individual is more likely to present a high level of CC (Goulet & and Singh, 2002).

The attitudes, behaviors, and norms of individuals relate to the trait dimensions of the Big Five Factor Model. Personality Traits are primary predictor variables in the proposed model.

Allport and his colleagues posited that personality traits are descriptive dimensions that describe and scale an individual's behavior (Allport, 1961). Because personality affects how a person acquires and processes information, they are closely associated with problem solving (Chamorro- Premuzic & Reichenbacher, 2008). The constellation of traits that characterize a person's behavior is referred to as personality. Consequently, personality theory is relevant to an understanding of problem solving ability.

An individual's perceptions of the difficulties inherent in a situation affect the existence of negative emotional states, such as anxiety and depression, and also the ability to manage them.

This has an impact on performance. Self-efficacy is reported to alleviate negative emotional states, and thereby enhance performance (Artino, LaRochelle, & Durning, 2010, Prat-Sala & Redford, 2010; Sawatzky, Ratner, Richardson, Washburn, Sudmant, & Mirwaldt, 2012). Self-efficacy is traditionally defined in terms of "belief in one's capabilities to organize and execute courses of action required to produce given attainments" (Bandura, 199, p. 191). It is not, however, a single construct. Bandura (199) defines different types of self-efficacy, defined by different functional situations.

General self-efficacy (GSE) is related to the general sense one has of one's ability to cope with daily activities and life events. Career self-efficacy (CSE), on the other hand, is related to one's ability to cope a particular career; in particular abilities to perform tasks related to career development, choice and adjustment (Anderson & Betz, 2001; Niles & Sowa, 1992). CSE provides important information relevant to understanding the complex career development process (Niles & Sowa, 1992) and is positively correlated with CC (Chang, 1996; Gboyega & Popoola, 2010). Consequently, I propose that CSE is a mediating variable in the model.

Unfortunately, there is no "one-size-fits-all" model of CSE, owing to differences between careers. Accordingly, I will modify an existing GSE scale for my study. This is discussed in more detail in Chapter 3.

The proposed study will test the conceptual model displayed in Figure 2. First, the model will test for associations between personality and thinking abilities. The relationships between thinking abilities and CSE will also be tested, as well as, the moderation of the perception of the problem environment on the association between thinking abilities and career- self efficacy. Finally, the proposed study will test the association between CSE and

CC, which is the principle dependent variable. Although the model will test for associations among variables, causality will be conceptually implied but not empirically demonstrated (Collier, Sekhon, & Stark, 2010).

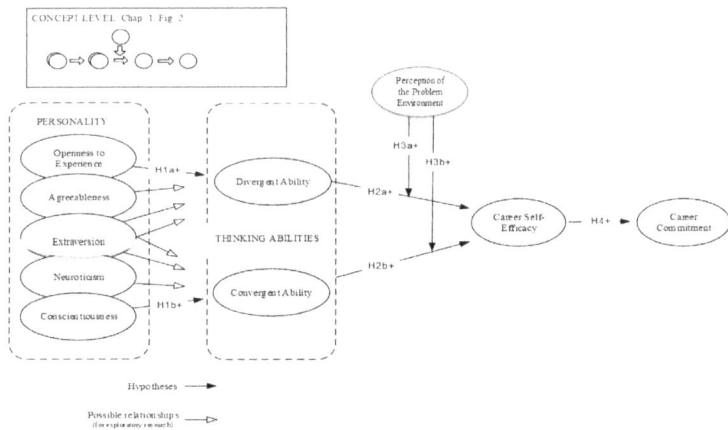

Figure 2. Path diagram of associations between personality and CC.

Section 5: Hypotheses Concerning Personality Traits and Thinking Abilities

The first two hypotheses, H_{1a} and H_{1b}, above, depict the relationships between personality traits and convergent and divergent thinking abilities. Two additional hypotheses, H_{2a} and H_{2b}, link thinking ability and CSE. The third set of hypotheses, H_{3a} and H_{3b}, depict the moderating effects of the perceived problem environment upon the correlations between thinking abilities and CSE. The final hypothesis, H_4, will test the association between CSE and CC.

I hypothesize positive associations between two personality traits, openness to experience and conscientiousness, and the two types of problem-related thinking ability, divergent and convergent thing ability. In

Figure 2, these are shown by arrows with solid heads. The three other personality traits, agreeableness, extraversion, and neuroticism, may have significant correlations with convergent and divergent ability; however, no hypotheses are proposed, and the correlations will be examined on an exploratory basis. These possible, but unsupported, associations are shown by arrows with open heads.

H$_{1a}$: Openness to Experience and Divergent Thinking Ability

Several studies have indicated that openness to experience is positively correlated with creativity (McCrae, 1987; Barrick & Mount, 2005; George & Zhou, 2001; King et al., 1996; LePine, Colquitt, & Erez, 2000). Other studies on personality and creativity indicate that higher levels of divergent thinking are associated with openness to experience (McCrae, 1987). The characteristics of people with the openness to experience trait are symptomatic of divergent rather than convergent thinking (McCrae, 1987). Chamorro-Premuzic and Reichenbacher (2008) similarly concluded that openness to experience facilitates divergent thinking. These results provide the rationale for *H$_{1a}$: Openness to Experience is positively correlated with divergent thinking ability.*

H$_{1b}$: Conscientiousness and Convergent Thinking Ability

There is empirical evidence to suggest that convergent problem solving requires conscientious application of established algorithms and procedures to well-defined problems. Le et al. (2011) suggested that highly conscientious employees may have difficulties with open problems that require divergent thinking, but they may be more suited to closed problems that require convergent thinking. Hyper-conscientious individuals with a high level of convergent thinking ability may be more skilled in the use of established logic or algorithms to address closed problems (Le et al., 2011). Chamorro-Premuzic and Furnham (2005) asserted that conscientiousness is not related to divergent thinking which suggests, albeit weakly, that if it's related to thinking ability in any way, then it is related to the other end of the spectrum, which is convergent ability. The evidence outlined above provides the rationale for H_{1b}: *Conscientiousness is positively correlated with convergent thinking ability.*

H_{2a}: Divergent Thinking and CSE

On the basis of the previous discussion, this study will argue that divergent thinking is a proxy for creativity, in that divergent thinking facilitates the creation of solutions (Guilford, 1967; Gomez-Mejia et al., 2007). Though divergent thinking is a proxy, there are implications for higher creativity. Jeon, Moon, and French (2011) found that "the role of task specific motivation in creative performance may be secondary to the role of creativity relevant cognitive abilities" (p. 68).

A large body of research has shown that creativity is positively correlated with CSE (Beghetto, 2006; Choi, 2004; Jaussi, Randel, & Dionne, 2007; Lim & Choi, 2009; Tierney & Farmer, 2010). Karwowski, Lebuda and Wiśniewska (2010) conducted a survey with 115 participants, which revealed statistically significant positive correlations between divergent thinking and the two scales developed to measure different aspects of creativity, creative self-efficacy and creative role-identity. Creativity facilitates problem-solving; further, those who are confident in their ability to solve problems will see their situation as more favorable and, as a result, will have greater self-efficacy. Because divergent thinking is closely related to creativity, we can rephrase that statement as H_{2a}: *Divergent thinking ability is positively correlated with CSE.*

H_{2b}: Convergent Thinking and CSE

Convergent thinking is used by an individual to identify and focus on the elements of a problem, gather the resources needed, and integrate the resources to arrive at a problem solution (Guilford, 1967; Gomez-Mejia et al, 2007). Convergent thinking has not been as extensively studied as divergent thinking, particularly as it relates to creativity and self-efficacy (Karwowski et al., 2010). Among the few studies that have focused on convergent thinking, Wigert (2012) confirmed that convergent thinking ability also facilitates creativity. Participants who were instructed to use processes consistent with convergent thinking, such as systematically listing alternatives, were more likely to generate creative solutions than those who were not so instructed. This suggests that those who use such processes automatically and consistently (i.e., those who exhibit convergent thinking) are likely to be better problem solvers. Marziano and Hefleblower (2011) also suggested that the ability to select the best course of action through convergent thinking may result in higher self-efficacy, supporting an argument similar to that offered for H_{3b} below. It follows that those who, on the basis of their past success solving problems, believe themselves to be competent problem solvers, are more likely to see a situation requiring problem solving favorable and, as a result, will have greater self-efficacy. This motivates H_{2a}: *Convergent thinking is positively correlated with CSE.*

H_{3a} and H_{3b}: Perception of the Problem Environment (open vs. closed) Moderates the Relationships between Thinking Abilities (Convergent vs. Divergent) and CSE.

Both hypotheses H_{3a} and H_{3b} rely upon the same logic: people are more confident of success in environments that favor their particular abilities. This confidence, in accordance with the TRA, supports an attitude that favors a particular decision; namely, the decision to remain in a chosen career. The research recounted here is concerned with the relationship between the environment and abilities; in particular, between the problems people encounter, and their thinking abilities.

Previous research has found that open problems that require an individual to use divergent thinking are more likely to encourage creative problem solving than closed problems, which do not prompt them to use varied approaches and types of reasoning (Kwon, Park, and Park, 2006). Other research has found that open problems were associated with increased confidence and optimism for participants who used divergent thinking (Colzato, Szapora, Lippelt & Hommel, n.d.). Confidence and optimism have been shown in past studies to be positively associated with CSE (Malik, 2013). These findings support H_{3a}: *An open problem environment will negatively moderate the association between divergent thinking ability and CSE.* By the same logic, we have H_{3b}: *A closed problem environment will positively moderate the association between convergent thinking ability and CSE.*

The signs of the interactions (positive or negative) will depend upon how the perception of the problem environment is operationalized. The PoPES scale, discussed elsewhere, will rank the environment on continuum ranging from open to closed. If we anticipate that larger values of the PoPES scale score correspond to more structured problems; to a more closed environment, and lower values to a more open environment, then H3a and H3b can be stated in the following alternative forms:

H_{3a}: *The correlation between divergent thinking ability and CC will be negatively correlated with PoPES: that is, stronger for lower (more open) values of the PoPES scale score.*

H_{3b}: *The correlation between convergent thinking ability and CC will be positively correlated with PoPES; that is, stronger for higher (more closed) values of the PoPES scale score.*

These two hypotheses are clearly speculative, but they are well-supported both by the TRA, and also common sense; we all prefer situations in which we are confident of thriving. They are also responsive to the call by Barrick, Mount and Judge (2001) for more theory and research into the behavioral implications of personality traits, which in this study is hypothesized to be antecedent to problem-relevant thinking abilities.

Extraversion, Agreeableness, and Neuroticism

As mentioned above, the roles of extraversion, agreeableness, and neuroticism, with respect to problem solving, will be analyzed in this study on an exploratory basis. There is some fragmentary evidence of possible correlations with thinking abilities.

H4: CSE and CC

The hypothesis relating CC with CSE (H4) is shown in Figure 2. CSE, defined as persons' beliefs in their abilities to perform tasks successfully, or accomplish work-related goals, is one of the most intensely explored concepts in psychology (Martochhio & Judge, 1997; Vancouver & Day, 2005). Much research has explored the association between CSE and creativity, and demonstrated that the two are positively correlated, and also correlated with favorable workplace outcomes (Beghetto, 2006; Cervone & Peake, 1986; Choi, 2004; Jaussi et al., 2007; Karwowski et al., 2010; Lim & Choi, 2009; Tierney & Farmer, 2002, 2010).

In addition, people with a stronger sense of CSE develop task strategies quickly and reach goals more efficiently (Locke & Latham, 2006). Individuals with greater CSE are also better able to cope with stressful situations in the workplace (Wallin, Bostrom, & Gustavsson, 2012). CSE is an essential motive for learning (Zimmerman, 2000). The Theory of Self- Efficacy posits that individuals with high levels of self-efficacy are more effective in their activities, because they are more convinced of their own capabilities to manage situations (Bandura, 1997). Furthermore, the Theory of Goal Setting posits that the successful completion of goals (implying how successful an individual will be in a particular problem environment) is necessary to maintain a high level of CSE (Locke & Latham, 2006). Since it is also reasonable to suppose that those with CSE perceive the workplace environment and believe in their abilities to solve job-specific problems as being favorable to achievement, the evidence presented above supports *H₄: CSE is positively correlated with CC.*

Summary

Because personality traits have been studied extensively for decades, they were the starting point for this research, which aimed to establish causal links between personality traits and CC, in the context of the types of problems that characterize work in that career. In the first section, I provided a general discussion of personality traits and their associations with behavior. The second section focused generally on thinking abilities and their associations with personality traits.

It is understood that careers involve choices and problems. A fundamental characteristic of any career, therefore, is the type of problems routinely faced by those pursuing that career. Accordingly, the third section defined the characteristics of a problem-solving environment, as perceived by those immersed in it; further, a new instrument was proposed for measuring those perceptions.

For this purpose, I borrowed a concept from GST, namely the concept of "open" versus "closed." A closed system has an impervious boundary around it and is independent of the environment; whereas an open system has a porous, or perhaps only a notional boundary around it, and is strongly influenced by the environment. Following this logic, I defined open problems as those influenced by many factors, and having no fixed rules for solving them, and closed problems as the converse. The perception of problem environment characterizes the environment in terms of the types of problems, either open or closed, that a person in that environment encounters.

The fourth section presents support for two hypotheses concerning the associations between personality traits and thinking abilities. Research findings indicated that openness to experience may be positively correlated with divergent thinking ability and the solving of open problems, because it covaries with curiosity, imagination, artistic interests, liberal attitudes, originality, and creativity. Conversely, conscientiousness is correlated against convergent thinking, which is related to the ability to identify a problem from a finite set of alternatives, sort through known solutions, and identify a solution. Extraversion, agreeableness, and neuroticism traits are not hypothesized to be related to convergent or divergent thinking abilities, but they will be analyzed in this study on an exploratory basis, and further research will be proposed as deemed appropriate. The fifth section supports the associations among CSE and CC with H_4.

Chapter 3 will describe the methods that will be used to test the hypotheses.

Hypotheses

H_{1a} Openness to Experience is positively correlated with divergent thinking ability.

H_{1b} Conscientiousness is positively correlated with convergent thinking ability.

H_{2a} Divergent thinking ability is positively correlated with CSE.

H_{2b} Convergent thinking ability is positively correlated with CSE.

H_{3a} 33An open problem environment will negatively moderate the association

between divergent thinking ability and CSE.

H_{3b} A closed problem environment will positively moderate the association between

convergent thinking ability and CSE.

H_4 CSE is positively correlated with CC.

CHAPTER 3

RESEARCH METHODOLOGY

Introduction

The purpose of this quantitative, cross-sectional study was to investigate the theoretical links between personality and CC by assessing the potentially mediating and moderating relationships between specific thinking abilities, perceptions of the problem environment, and CSE. This chapter contained information regarding the research design, population, constructs and measurement instruments, statistical methods, and limitations and ethical considerations. In particular, this chapter summarized the methodology used to address the following research question: Do job-specific problems and individual problem-solving abilities mediate the relationship between personality and CC? The proposed research methodology addressed the ancillary research questions in Chapter 1 and the hypotheses outlined in Chapter 2.

Research Design

This project utilized a cross-sectional, correlational design to test the theoretical links between personality and CC. This study used standard survey methods (i.e., using fixed- response self-report instruments to collect cross-sectional data), which were used to test the hypotheses using standard multivariate statistical techniques (Kline, 2010; Monecke & Leisch, 2012). During the data collection phase, the results of preliminary analyses were used to assess the state of the obtained data, including testing of statistical assumptions, as well as testing the simple, bivariate relationships.

In order to evaluate the potentially moderating and/or mediating relationships between personality and CC through CSE, a series of partial least squared structural equation models (PLS-SEM) were tested. The PLS-SEM allowed the evaluation of relationships between latent, or unobserved, variables. Rooted in the review of the literature presented in Chapter 2, I tested the hypotheses using PLS-SEM. Although each hypothesis was presented as a single predictive statement, this did not imply that each hypothesis would be tested in isolation. Each hypothesis was an integral part of a structural equation model, proposing predictive relationships between a system that integrates personality traits and CC. It was more informative to test the hypotheses as parts of an inter-related system, rather than individually.

The proposed research examined the relationships between self-reported personality traits and CC at the individual, rather than the team or organizational level of analysis. The focus on the individual level built on a prior body of research on individual differences in personality traits, cognitive processes, and CC. The results of the research are applicable to matching employees to appropriate jobs depending on the match between levels of conscientiousness and demands for convergent and divergent problem solving, or for using training and consulting to address potential discrepancies between individual employee traits and the problem-solving requirements of the job that they occupy. This research study could potentially address an individual's propensity to solve problems and how that may prove useful to organizations as they design policies and procedures to improve the quality of their selection and hiring of the best fit of personnel to their organization. Although the emphasis on the individual level of analysis has some benefits, it also imposed certain limitations. It is important to note that studies have examined the relationship between personality traits and job performance at the team level.

Illustratively, research on personality and CC has been used to create teams composed of members with complementary traits. Turel and Zhang (2010) suggested that teams can be formed of members with different personality traits that complement, supplement, or otherwise create combinations that enhance the performance of the team.

Study Population and Power

The target population consisted of participants belonging to various educational backgrounds, careers, and socioeconomic backgrounds. The results of the study were interpreted to predict which people, as characterized by specific personality traits, are more or less likely to be committed to particular careers, those careers being characterized by the types of problems that they typically encounter. Inclusion criteria included participants being 18 years or older, able to understand English and read at the 5th grade level, being a US citizen and whether the participant is located in the US. Further, in order to achieve a population diverse enough to distinguish between those who are more adept at solving open or closed problems, a representative sample of US participants over the age of 18 years old was recruited.

Using the online calculator at https://www.checkmarket.com/market-research- resources/sample-size-calculator/ (CheckMarket, 2015) (See Figure 3), the sample size needed to achieve a 5% margin of error around the responses to the survey instruments, was determined to reflect the representative sample of the population in the study.

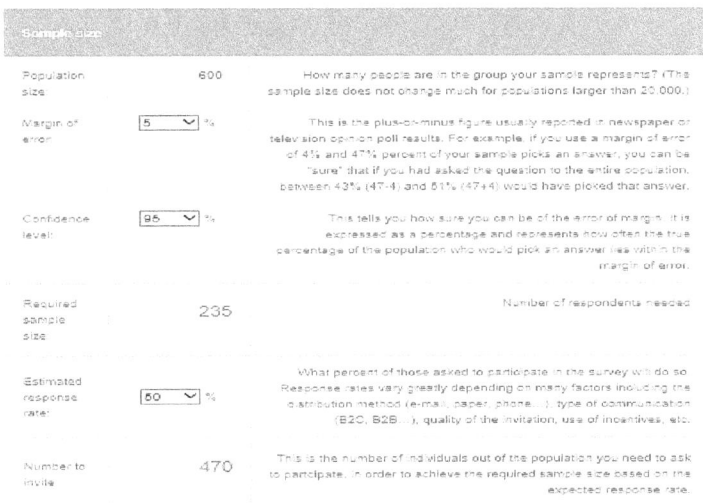

Figure 3. Sample size calculation (CheckMarket, 2015)

The sampling procedure yielded a targeted sample of 286 respondents as 490 participants selected to take the survey. Historically, response rates to online surveys are low, averaging about 25% (Kaplowitz, Hadlock, & Levine, 2004); however, more recent research suggests an improvement. The response rate was greater than 50% and did not require re-evaluation of the survey items within the primary study.

The sampling frame consisted of lists obtained from cooperating entities. A total of 286 were found to be eligible. The participants were expected to be willing to participate in the survey, not just for educational purposes, but also to contribute to research that is linked to their interests. All individuals who volunteered to participate were accepted; however, participants were excluded when/if they answered "no" to the inclusion criteria and/or if they are under the age of 18. If the participant was "under 18", they were taken to a disqualification page within the survey.

In comparison to covariance based (CB)-SEM, PLS-SEM was considered to be a more robust analysis technique due to having a smaller sample size (Reinartz, Haenlein, & Henseler, 2009). As a comparison, power analysis with CB-SEM was based on the statistical power of the specific model being tested and minimum sample sizes generally range from 200-800, depending greatly on the complexity of the specific model (Chin & Newsted, 1999). Conversely, with

PLS-SEM, power is a function of the number of manifest and latent variables (Chin & Newsted, 1999). With PLS-SEM, the general recommendation on sample size for ensuring sufficient power ranges from 30-100 (Sarstedt, Ringle, Henseler, & Hair, 2014).

Data Collection Tools & Procedures

Survey Sampling International (SSI), a data solutions and technology company, was used to recruit the target population. The survey tool allowed the researcher to select targeting criteria which ensured the customization of the target audience. This ensured participants were demographically and culturally diverse, as well as, a representative of the United States population.

The following steps were followed to conduct the online survey. Data collection was completed in two phases, whereby an online pilot study of 133 participants were asked to complete the Perception of the Problem Environment Scale (PoPES) and modified General Self-Efficacy (GSE) instruments. After administering the pilot survey, any deficiencies in the design of the PoPES or modified GSE, were addressed and updated in the main survey. The pilot study validated the instruments used in the primary study. In the primary study, approximately 286 participants were asked to complete the Big Five Instrument (BFI), Remote Associates Test (RAT), Alternate Uses Test (AUT), and Career Commitment Measure (CCM), as well as, a few demographic questionnaires. For both the pilot and primary study, the data collection procedures were detailed, along with the findings in Chapter 4.

Recruitment. Participants were recruited using a panelist company, Survey Sampling International, LLC (SSI). Eligibility to participate included being able to understand English and read at the 5th grade reading level, being a US citizen, located in the US, 18 years of age or older, and currently employed. Other than the criteria listed above, no other participant groups were targeted for this study. Panelist participants voluntarily enrolled with the panelist company to be prospective participants and were compensated by the panelist company and not the individual researcher. If participants were found eligible to participate in this study, they earned points for participation according to the Panel Rewards Terms and Conditions approved by SSI. These points were credited to their panelist account by SSI at the conclusion of the study. Their participation was strictly voluntary. Eligible participants were invited by online messaging. The recruitment message included information about the topic and title of the survey, as well as, the online link for the survey. PsychData housed the online survey tool. Participants were asked to respond within 3 weeks, after which time the online survey was closed. As recommended by Yoon and Horne (2004), 3 weeks was found to be sufficient time to increase the likelihood of respondent's participating in the survey and potentially reducing the nonresponse rate.

Informed consent. Before clicking on the survey link the panelist company asked participants to provide their panelist participant ID number; however, this information was not stored or shared with the researcher and was only used to verify their eligibility as a panelist participant. Upon clicking on the link to the survey (i.e., pilot or primary study), participants were given informed consent (see Appendix A). Participants were told that participation was completely voluntary and that they could stop participating at any point in time. If participants declined to participate, they were not allowed to continue participation in the survey. All participants who signed the informed consent were assigned a random unique respondent ID that was not linked with any identifying contact information or personal identifying information. The unique respondent ID, therefore, served as a record to the researcher that the participant signed the informed consent. Once participants indicated that they agreed to be a participant, they were taken to the survey itself, whereby they were asked six inclusion criteria questions (see Appendix A). If participants indicated that they could not understand English, read at or above the 5th grade level, were not a US citizen, whether they were located in the US, were under the age of 18 years, or not employed, they were not allowed to continue participation in the survey.

Pilot study. Participants completing the pilot study were asked to complete the PoPES and modified GSE instruments, which consisted of an initial 14 and 10 items respectively. This survey was housed in a separate survey link from the primary study. Participants who completed the pilot study were thanked for their participation and given the contact information of the researcher should they have any additional questions. After all pilot data was collected, the researcher performed a factor analysis and dropped items from the survey that did not statistically load well. The findings of the pilot study are covered in detail in Chapter 4.

Primary study. After the conclusion of the pilot study, a separate survey link was sent out to prospective participants. Participants who clicked on the link were shown the informed consent (see above). Participants were asked to complete the BFI (John, Naumann, & Soto (2008), which consisted of 10 items. Then they completed the RAT (Mednick & Mednick (1967) which consisted of 10 questions. Then they completed the AUT (Guilford, Christensen, Merrifield, & Wilson (1978), which consisted of three (3) items (3 items with six (6) subcomponents (i.e., 1 Common Object and 6 (a-f) answers or uses)). Then they completed the PoPES (original contribution to the proposed study), which consisted of 20 items which was increased by 6 questions based on data analysis of the pilot study, and this is addressed in detail in Chapter 4. Then they completed the modified GSE (Schwarzer & Jerusalem (1995), which consisted of 10 items. Then, they completed the CCM (Carson & Bedeian (1994), which consisted of 10 items. They then completed a few demographic questions. At the conclusion of the survey, participants were thanked for their participation and given the contact information of the researcher should they have any questions. None of the participants contacted the researcher.

Data validation. During the survey collection process, data was monitored to ensure that respondents were providing valid responses. Participants who provided inconsistent demographic responses with the inclusion criteria questions were flagged as being potentially invalid. For example, participants who reported "yes" that they were currently employed at the onset of the study and then reported that they were unemployed at the conclusion of the study were flagged as a suspicious respondent.

Confidentiality. Participants provided informed consent by responding to the question above. No identifying information was shared with the researcher. The panelist company used the participants' ID number to verify participants' identify; however, no contact information or identifying information was shared in the data or with the researcher. Data downloaded from the online survey tool included a unique respondent ID that was used by the online tool to verify the record of participation. However, this unique respondent ID number was not connected to any identifying information. Participants were reminded at the beginning of the study that their information was completely anonymous and no participant identifiers would be stored.

Variables and Measurement Instruments

The variables were generated by averaging item responses, as shown in Table 2. An initial descriptive analysis was conducted of the variables, using the protocols described by Field (2009) including the frequency distributions of the responses to the Demographic Questionnaire, in order to provide a demographic profile of the participants.

Measurement Quality Assessment

Prior to testing the theorized model, the measurement model was examined to ensure the quality of the model. Additionally, the average variance extracted (AVE), composite reliability (CR), and internal consistency (expressed as Cronbach's α) were evaluated based on the recommendations of Fornell and Larcker (1981), Kline (2011), and Nunnally and Bernstein (1994). Based on these recommendations, latent constructs with averages approaching or beyond the critical value of .500 were retained in the model. Discriminant validity was examined by evaluating the correlations among latent constructs to ensure that all correlations were below the critical threshold of .85, thus demonstrating that there did not appear to be redundancy in the indicators and the overall model.

Table 2

Operational Definitions of Variables

Variable	Operational Definition
Conscientiousness	Responses to relevant items of the BFI, with a response set ranging from 1, Disagree Strongly, to 5, Agree Strongly. The higher the score, the higher the level of conscientiousness.
Openness to Experience	As above, using BFI items relevant to openness to experience.
Extraversion	As above, using BFI items relevant to extraversion.
Agreeableness	As above, using BFI items relevant to agreeableness.
Neuroticism	As above, using BFI items relevant to neuroticism.
Convergent Thinking Ability	Fluency, measured by RAT as the total number of responses describing different possible uses for an object, using an open-ended format. The higher the score, the higher the level of convergent thinking ability.
Divergent Thinking Ability	Sum of scores for a 20-item test in the AUT consisting of words presented in stimulus groups of three. Participants are required to recall a word that can be related to each of the three stimulus items. The higher the score, the higher the level of divergent thinking ability.

Perception of Problem Environment Scale	Sum of scores of responses to the 20 items in the proposed scale; 20 items with a 6-point scale, ranging from 1, Strongly Disagree, to 6, Strongly Agree; The higher the score, the more open is the subject's perception of the problem environment.
Career Commitment	Measured using the 12-item CC scale. Three-components are measured (career identity, career resilience, and career planning). Measured using a 7-point disagree – agree scale. The higher the score, the higher the level of career identity and commitment.
Career Self-Efficacy	Measured using the GSE scale which has been modified to meet the particular requirements of the context of this particular research. Response ranges are made on a 4-point scale from 1, Not at all true, to 4, Exactly true. Sum up the responses to all 10 items provides a scoring range from 10 to 40 and requires no recoding. The higher the score, the higher the CSE.

Table 3

Constructs and Instruments

Construct(s)	Instruments
Personality traits	Big Five Inventory (BFI)
Thinking abilities	Convergent ability: Remote Associations Test (RAT)
	Divergent ability: Alternative Uses Test (AUT)
Perception of Problem Environment	Perception of Problem Environment Scale (PoPES)
Career Self-Efficacy	General Self-Efficacy (GSE)
Career Commitment	Career Commitment Measure (CCM)
Demographics	Various demographic items

Measurement of Personality

The personality construct was difficult to operationalize in quantitative terms because many internal and external factors and processes, along with many facets, influence it. There are several sophisticated assessment tests, tools, and scales that provide insight into an individual's personality, including their attitudes, behaviors, and motivations towards their job performance. Gidron, Koehler, and Tversky (1993) used "a metric of behavioral quantification rather than discrete categories" to distinguish among traits (p. 594). Englert (2008) used the widely known Neuroticism-Extraversion-Openness (NEO) Personality Inventory (NEO-PI), a self-report instrument, to quantify personality. For the purposes of this study, the normal 240-item inventory assessing the five major dimensions of an individual's personality were not used; instead, the short, 10-item Big Five Inventory (BFI) instrument was used, as described below.

In this study, the researcher operationalized conscientiousness, openness to experience, extraversion, agreeableness, and neuroticism as subject responses on the five sub-scales of the Big Five Inventory (John, Donahue, & Kentle, 1991; Rammstedt & John, 2007; John, Naumann, & Soto, 2008, Costa & McCrae, 1985). The psychometric properties of this assessment tool have been well established. John et al. (1991) reported the test-retest-reliability of the BFI was high (r = .75 to .90) and the internal consistency reliability of the scales was good (Cronbach's alpha ≥ .85). Evidence for the convergent validity of the BFI comes from studies reporting that the BFI scale scores are highly correlated with other indices of major personality traits in ways that are consistent with the Big Five Model of Personality (Le et al., 2011).

The BFI used a self-reported assessment of characteristics associated with traits (see Appendix B). The respondent replied to 10 items concerning *How I am in general,* indicating the degree of applicability of each. Traits were operationalized as the mean scores of related items. The BFI differs from cognitive-behavioral assessments of personality characteristics that focus on situations (rather than traits) leading to particular response patterns. For example, the Assertive Behavior Survey Schedule (ABSS) requires the respondent to endorse specific situations that call for assertiveness (Kaplan & Saccuzzo, 2010). Cognitive-behavioral assessments, however, measure states and not traits (e.g., respondents may be assertive in certain situations, but not others); consequently, cognitive-behavioral assessments were not applicable to this study, which focused on traits and temporary states.

Measurement of Thinking Abilities

The researcher operationalized convergent thinking ability as subject responses on the Remote Associates Test (RAT). The RAT was first conceptualized by Professor Sarnoff Mednick in 1962 and developed by Mednick and Mednick (1967). The RAT is a 20-item test consisting of words presented in stimulus groups of three, and respondents are required to recall one word that can be directly related all three of the stimulus words (see Appendix C).

The researcher operationalized divergent thinking ability as subject responses to the Alternative Uses Test (AUT), which was originally designed by Guilford (1967) and subsequently developed by Guildford, Christensen, Merrifield, and Wilson (1978). The AUT measures an individual's ability to come up with as many uses as possible for ten common household objects, using an open-ended response format (see Appendix D). The AUT consisted of four sub-categories: fluency, originality, flexibility, and elaboration. This study examined each of the subscales, especially the fluency subscale (i.e., the total number of responses generated by the participant) because this subscale has been found to be predictive of multiple indicators of divergent problem solving skill (Bately & Furnham, 2008). Both the RAT and the AUT are reported to exhibit high levels of internal consistency reliability (Cronbach's alpha $\geq$ .7) and high convergent validity with other assessments of problem-solving ability. The RAT and AUT have both been used extensively in research on divergent and convergent problem solving (e.g., Farah, Haim, Sankoorikal & Chatterjee, 2009; Jones, Caulfield, Wilkinson & Weller, 2011).

Measurement of the Perception of the Problem Environment

To measure perception of the problem environment, the PoPES was used. The PoPES (see Appendix E), a 20-item inventory, measured to what extent individuals perceived their problem-solving environment as being along an open vs closed continuum as described in Chapter 2. Perception of the problem environment is distinct from other types of individual difference measures, such as the Decision Making Individual Differences Inventory (DMIDI) (Appelt, Milch, Handgraaf, & Weber, 2011). Although this measure examined to what extent individuals approached and solved problems, it did not examine the extent to which individuals perceive problems as being open or closed.

Because there is limited information about this construct in the organizational behavior literature, the PoPES was developed to specifically target the perception of the problem environment and not necessarily the job variety. With this scale, the researcher investigated whether there was a relationship to either actual problem solving propensity (people's comfort level in solving problems) or actual problem solving ability (whether they can get a useful result for a problem). The intent of the scale was to consider the intrinsic nature of problems and understand what goes on in problem solver's heads and how well they actually solve problems. It also helped to determine how comfortable they are with solving problems.

This proposed inventory was broken down into three sections. The 20-questions used a 6-point response format ranging from Strongly Disagree to Strongly Agree with no neutral option (i.e., Neither Agree nor Disagree). The neutral response option is avoided, because it would have provided an easy answer for subjects who have difficulty making up their minds (Kaplan & Saccuzzo, 2010). The neutral option was originally devised for market research, in eliciting opinions about intentions to purchase a particular product. It is reasonable to assume that some respondents will have a genuinely neutral attitude towards a certain product if they know little about its usability or performance (Aaker, Kumar, & Day, 2001).

The odd numbered items in the Perception of the Problem Environment Scale correspond to experiences in a closed problem solving environment (e.g., In my line of work, the problems I encounter on the job...1... can be solved using known rules; 3... are relatively easy to understand and solve. The odd numbered items are scored from 1 = Strongly Agree to 6 = Strongly Disagree. The one-dimensional scale was operationalized by adding the scores for the 20 items.

The proposed scale was piloted with a small number of participants. This allowed for a closer examination of the mechanics and functionality of the survey and the instructions, structure, and design of it were assessed. Utilizing SSI (2016), the survey and reminder emails were sent to up to 177 participants. This number of participants supported the psychometric soundness of the proposed scale. A factor analysis was conducted to ensure that those questions loading the strongest are kept in the final survey. The participants had 2 weeks to respond. The procedure terminated after 2 weeks.

At this point, it is worthwhile to recapitulate some points concerning the origin, development, and meaning of the perception of the problem environment scale (PoPES). PoPES attempts to quantify the individual's *perception* of the problem environment, which may not be isomorphic with the *actual* problem environment (assuming the latter is, in some sense, objectively real and measurable). But although it is a perception, it is not *merely* a perception;

rather, it actually is the environment, as it appears to the individual. In accordance with the Theory of Reasoned Action, it is a factor that enters the individual's assessment of whether certain behaviors will achieve desired outcomes.

When designing the PoPES, I used the theoretical framework of the General Systems Theory which classified systems as open vs. closed. In GST, an open system has poorly defined boundaries. It is affected by many factors, some quite remote from the processes central to the system. A closed system has well-defined boundaries, and is not affected, or only weakly affected, by exogenous factors. Similarly; an "open" problem environment is characterized by "many moving parts," ambiguity and lack of structure; a "closed" environment by simplicity, rules and a well-defined structure. Again, this is an individual perception, and a basis for individual decisions.

When designing the PoPES items, I began by imagining how an open versus closed environment would appear, in terms of observed job characteristics. For example, problems that typically "require imagination" would characterize an open, rather than a closed, system.

Whether certain problems actually *do* require imagination is moot; in a rule-bound profession such as policing, such problems may be rare. However, it is the individual's perception of the environment that is being measured, not the actual environment, and it is the individual's perceptions that determine his or her decisions.

Would different people perceive the same environment differently? If so, what are the covariates of those differences? These are interesting questions, but beyond the scope of the present research, which did not control for actual environment, but instead recruited respondents having many different jobs.

Measurement of CSE

Self-efficacy is "belief in one's capabilities to organize and execute courses of action required, producing given attainments" (Bandura, 1997, p. 191). Generalized Self Efficacy (GSE) is viewed as "a trait like construct" (Imam, Rahman, Julita, Hafiz, 2011, p. 1). The scale is used broadly and globally. It is used for a variety of demands in an individual's life.

Additionally, Chen, Gully, and Eden (2009) explained that "…GSE captures differences among individuals in their tendency to view themselves as capable of meeting task demands in a broad array of contexts" (p.63).

Career Self-Efficacy (CSE), on the other hand, is related to one's capacities with respect to a particular career. There is no all-purpose CSE scale, yet that is what is needed in the present instance. CSE is hypothesized to be a predictor of CC, so the CSE scale needed to be oriented towards career attainments rather than overall life attainments, yet it did not need to be oriented towards any particular career. I constructed an adhoc CSE scale that met these requirements by modifying the Generalized Self Efficacy Scale (GSE) (Schwarzer & Jerusalem, 1995; Appendix F).

Individuals with higher CSE set more ambitious objectives and have higher expectations of their ability to perform. Conversely, those with low CSE set easy objectives, focusing on their failings and the perceived difficulties of a situation. High levels of motivation are associated with high levels of CSE, as are positive emotional states. All of these factors are linked to an individual's ability to perceive and manage negative emotional states (e.g., stress, anxiety, and depression) with an associated impact on performance. CSE is reported to alleviate negative emotional states, and thereby enhance performance (Artino, LaRochelle, & Durning, 2010, Prat-Sala & Redford, 2010; Sawatzky, Ratner, Richardson, Washburn et al, 2012).

Measurement of Career Commitment

Career commitment is a broad multidimensional concept, underpinned by Career Motivation Theory (London, 1983), and defined in terms of the strength of an individual's motivation to work in a chosen career role. Chang (1999) found that CC has a significant influence on organizational commitment and turnover intention. Several dimensions of CC have been identified including (a) individual needs, interests, abilities and personality traits potentially relevant to promoting an individual's career; and (b) situational or work-related environment factors that influence motivation, such as leadership styles and professional development programs (Goulet & Singh, 2002). Because this specific concept of commitment was most relevant to my study, I chose it as the dependent variable. CC was measured using the 12-item Career Commitment Measure (CCM) developed by Carson and Bedeian (1994) listed in Appendix G.

Measurement of Demographic & Control Variables

This study included demographic items, specifically age and gender. I used two measurement scales, the RAT and AUT respectively to assess convergent and divergent thinking abilities. Previous studies using the RAT and AUT indicated that the capacity for convergent and divergent thinking may vary with demographic factors, including age (McCrae, Arenberg, & Costa, 1987) and gender (Kuhn & Holling, 2009). This information ensured a reasonable representation of participants. Goldberg (1998) found that demographic variables were associated with personality dimensions. He found that demographic variable may moderate the variance between other personality traits and a predictor of an individual's performance.

Table 4

Functional Definitions of Variables and Instruments Used to Measure the Variables

Variable	Functional Definition	Instrument	Reference	Appendix
Informed Consent	NA	NA	This study	A*
Conscientiousness and Openness to Experience	Predictor Variable	Big Five Inventory (BFI)	John, Naumann, & Soto (2008)	B
Convergent Thinking Ability	Predictor Variable	Remote Associates Test (RAT)	Mednick & Mednick (1967)	C
Divergent Thinking Ability	Predictor Variable	Alternative Uses Test (AUT)	Guilford, Christensen, Merrifield, & Wilson (1978)	D

Perception of the Problem Environment	Moderating Variable	Perception of the Problem Environment Scale (PoPES)	This study	E
Career Self-Efficacy	Mediating Variable	Generalized Self-Efficacy Scale (GSE) (modified)	Schwarzer & Jerusalem (1995)	F
Career Commitment	Dependent Variable	Career Commitment Measure (CCM)	Carson & Bedeian (1994)	G
Age, Gender Years of Experience Education Level	Controlling Variables	Demographic Questionnaire	This study	H

*Appendix A is the Informed Consent; the pilot and primary consent forms are both Appendix A.

Statistical Analysis

Preliminary analyses. Preliminary analyses were used to assess univariate normality and multicollinearity, which are required for estimating an SEM model. To check assumptions of univariate normality, skewness and kurtosis values of observed variables were investigated.

Overall, absolute kurtosis values of more than 3.0 can affect the fit of the SEM (Kline, 2011). The correlation coefficients, tolerance, and variance inflation factor (VIF) were inspected to check for multicollinearity issues. Correlation estimates of ≥ .85, tolerance values < .10, and/or VIFs of > 10 at the multivariate level may indicate the presence of a multicollinearity problem in the SEM (Kline, 2011). This preliminary assessment determined if data transformations or bootstrapping was necessary. Reliability analyses were conducted utilizing Cronbach's α to test the internal consistency of instruments. There is more information on the statistical analyses for both the pilot and primary study in Chapter 4.

Structural Model Analysis. The SEM is a recommended statistical technique for personality research (Shimmack et al., 2009). SEM is a second generation method that offers many advantages over first generation techniques developed nearly 100 years ago, such as multiple regression. SEM provided (a) the ability to analyze, simultaneously, the relationships between multiple predictor and outcome variables; (b) flexible theoretical assumptions (e.g., multicollinearity is tolerated); (c) the facility to operationalize mediating and moderating variables; and (d) the use a graphic user interface to construct path diagrams and visualize the hypothesized relationships (Alavifar, Karimimalayer, & Annuar, 2012). The SEM involved factor analysis and path analysis. The first stage was to examine the measurement model using confirmatory factor analysis. Next, the measurement model was defined as the relationships between (a) the indicators (e.g., the item scores measured using questionnaires) and the (b) the latent variables (i.e., the constructs that cannot be measured directly, but they can be operationalized by combining indicators using factor analysis).

The second stage was to evaluate the structural model using path analysis, which involved computation and interpretation of the path coefficients and effect sizes between the latent variables (Kline, 2010). Two SEM techniques were considered for this study: (a) CB-

SEM or partial least squares-based structural equation modeling (PLS-SEM). I chose PLS-SEM because it has less restrictive data requirements than CB-SEM. PLS is not as sensitive as CB- SEM to the measurement levels and distributional characteristics of the data. PLS does not require normally distributed variables measured at the interval level. As previously discussed, the sample size requirements for CB-SEM are extremely stringent. Westland (2010) suggested that over 80% of research articles based on the use of CB-SEM drew false conclusions due to insufficient sample sizes. In contrast, sample size considerations are not so important when using PLS-SEM (Hair et al., 2010; 2011), and is generally considered acceptable in samples of 50 or greater. PLS is a described as a soft modeling technique because it makes minimum demands on the data and the researcher, in comparison to hard techniques, such as CB-SEM and multiple regression which are much more difficult to implement in practice (Monecke & Leisch, 2012). In PLS-SEM, path coefficients indicate the absolute magnitude of direct and indirect effects between latent constructs. Path coefficients are interpreted as follows: |~.10| indicates a small effect, |~.30| indicates a moderate effect, and |>.50| indicates a large effect (Cohen, 1988).

Limitations

Correlation and Causation

The main limitations of this study, as described in Chapter 2, were as follows. First, this was a cross-sectional correlational study that established the existence or direction of cause and effect relationships (Pearl,

2009). Further, self-report data is not 100% accurate. Although self- report data may be suspect to socially desirable responding, previous research has shown that self-report data only differs slightly from other methods of personality assessment (e.g., interviews or informants) (Roberts, 2011). Compared to CB-SEM, PLS-SEM is inherently less robust at fully accounting for co-variances across indicators and constructs); however, PLS-SEM is still a robust procedure for testing theoretical models (Ringle, Sarstedt, & Straub, 2012); however, PLS-SEM is a 21st century method that is less sensitive to sample size than conventional covariance based structural equation modeling (CB-SEM); Hair, Ringle, & Sarstedt, 2011; Jannoo, Yap, Auchoybur, & Lazim, 2014)). Furthermore, PLS computed model parameters by bootstrapping. Up to 1000 repeated random sub-samples were drawn from the sample data, in order to compute the PLS model parameters. Consequently, a random sample does not need to be drawn from the target population in order to conduct PLS-SEM. Also, there may be confounding variables that may affect the variations in the independent and dependent variables of the study (McDonald, 2014). The participants were randomly selected, and the control of the research design and multivariate statistical analyses prevented this (Aschengrau & Seage, 2009).

Internal Validity

There was also a possibility that the internal validity of the study may have been threatened by response bias. Response bias is a general term for a wide range of issues that prevent participants in surveys from offering full and truthful responses. Response bias is inevitably a problem in research that involves collecting data using self-report questionnaires. Personality assessments based on self-report instruments may sometimes be prone to response bias, depending on the proclivities of the participants (Paulhus, 1991; Paulhus & John, 1998). Consequently, a consideration of the possible impact of response bias is essential to aid the interpretation of the results of this study.

External Validity

There is the possibility that the external validity of this study was threatened by sampling bias, meaning that the results may not necessarily be generalized from the sample to the population, because the purposive sample is not representative of the target population in all of its essential characteristics (Creswell, 2009). Under-representation or over-representation of some groups of participants may occur if recruitment is based on self-selection (Bethlehem 2010). The frequencies of the demographic groups in the study sample was compared with the frequencies of the demographic groups in the target population (using information about the population in the database on gender, age, and level) in an attempt to identify possible sample bias due to self-selection.

Potential Bias

Social desirability bias refers to the tendency of some respondents to answer questionnaire items falsely, in a manner that makes themselves and/or their organizations look good, rather than to provide accurate and truthful answers. Social desirability bias usually takes the form of respondents consistently over-reporting "good" behavior and under-reporting or evading "bad" behavior (Holtgreaves, 2004). Some respondents may have deliberately emphasized desirable issues, and purposely neglected adverse issues, because they want to safeguard their jobs or protect the interests of their organization (Zikmund, Babin, Carr, & Griffin, 2010).

Acquiescent response bias is the tendency of some respondents to give positive, agreeable, or optimistic answers to most questionnaire items, irrespective of whether or not they actually do endorse the items in reality. Extreme response bias could also be a limitation. This refers to the propensity of some respondents to consistently provide polarized answer patterns, at one or the other end of the scale of questionnaire items (Paulhus, 1991).

There are a number of reasons participants could have potentially provided biased responses, including (a) they are naturally very polite and respectful people, who prefer to avoid any type of argument or social risk-taking, so they provide responses which they think will gratify the researcher; (b) they perceive themselves to be of lower educational and/or social status than the researcher, and so they defer to her authority by endorsing what they think she believes to be true; (c) they do not respond to the items according to their own individual perceptions, but follow the collective perceptions or norms of their own group or culture; and (d) they are too busy, distracted, or bored to provide responses that reflect their own individual perceptions, so they mindlessly provide random responses to all of the items (Paulhus, 1991).

Because the subjects were, to the greatest extent possible, drawn from academics, students and working professionals, who are guaranteed anonymity, it was less likely that the responses would be biased (Creswell, 2009). Furthermore, response bias were, to some extent, reduced by statistical analysis. According to measurement theory, the process of compositing reliably measured questionnaire item scores reinforces the valid and reliable components of a latent variable, at the same time as cancelling out the bias caused by inconsistent and erroneous responses (Allen & Yen, 2002). The consistency and uniformity of the item scores did not, however, imply that the latent variables measure the truth, because there was the possibility that all the respondents could provide consistently incorrect answers.

Confidentiality and Ethical Assurance

The confidentiality of all participants was respected. No information that could be used to identify the respondents was disseminated. Participating in this study did not pose any mental, physical, or environmental risk to the participants. No unethical deceptive or coercive techniques were used. No person was forced to participate, and no respondent was excluded on the basis of their gender, age, race, or any other characteristics.

CHAPTER 4

DATA ANALYSIS AND RESULTS

Introduction

The purpose of this dissertation was to examine the structural pathways of factors leading to CC. More specifically, it aimed to examine how personality styles impacts CC through specific thinking abilities, perceptions of the problem environment and career-related self-efficacy. This chapter will provide a description of the analytic procedures, starting with pilot testing, followed by the preliminary (i.e., bivariate) and primary analyses (i.e., multivariate) analyses. Particular attention was be given to the structural model assessing the overall theorized model as it pertains to answering the specific research hypotheses, which are:

Table 5

Summary of Research Hypotheses

H1a	Openness to Experience is positively correlated with divergent thinking ability.
H1b	Conscientiousness is positively correlated with convergent thinking ability.
H2a	Divergent thinking ability is positively correlated with CSE.
H2b	Convergent thinking ability is positively correlated with CSE.
H3a	An open problem environment will negatively moderate the association between divergent thinking ability and CSE.
H3b	A closed problem environment will positively moderate the association between convergent thinking ability and CSE.
H4	CSE is positively correlated with CC.

The practical purpose of this research is to assist researchers and practitioners in examining conceptually how the Big Five personality traits of Conscientiousness and Openness to Experience are related to convergent and divergent thinking abilities. Furthermore, it aimed to examine Conscientiousness and Openness to Experience as related to self-efficacy, as moderated by the perceived characteristics of the problem solving environment. Lastly, it will examine how these relationship impact CC, within the context of thinking abilities and the perception of the problem environment.

Pilot Study

Prior to conducting the primary study, a pilot study was conducted for two scales used in this study, the PoPES and GSE. The goal of the pilot was to assess the factor structure of items, and there needed to be sufficient sample size to conduct the exploratory factor analysis and assess reliability of the instrument(s). Data was collected in the pilot study anonymously via on-line questionnaires using the online panelist, SSI and housed by PsychData.

Initial Data Screening. For the pilot study, 177 participants consented to participate in the study. After screening the data for participant eligibility, 27 (15.3%) participants were excluded from the analysis for not meeting eligibility criteria. Among the 27 participants excluded, 7 reported that they were not employed, 9 were not located in the US, and 11 did not provide eligibility information and/or ended participation in the survey (i.e., the remaining survey items were left blank). Among the remaining 150 participants, 17 (9.6%) were removed due to careless responding. According to Huang, Curran, Keeney, Poposki, and DeShon (2012), respondents should be removed from analyses who do not meet criteria for attentive responding. Specifically, 14 cases were removed because their responses did not vary across survey items (i.e., item variance = 0.00), two cases were removed because their reported year of birth did not match their reported age category, and one case was removed because they took longer than 1 hour to complete the survey. The final pilot sample consisted of 133 participants (60 men, 73 women; M_{age} = 41.45, SD_{age} = 13.56).

Perception of the Problem Environment. Pearson's correlation coefficients were calculated among all 14 items. The results revealed that the items were small-to-moderately correlated with no negative correlations among items, and this lent itself to exploration of a complex problem environment. An exploratory factory analysis using varimax rotation was conducted on all 14 items.

Because the Pearson's correlations did not reveal negative correlations among items, items were not reverse-coded prior to conducting the factor analysis. The results revealed that four separate factors with eigenvalues greater than 1.00 accounted for 64.6% of the total variance among items. One item, "require careful attention to limits (budget, time, schedule)," was considered for removal due to low factor loadings and loading on more than one factor. After removing the item, the final model consisted of the same four factors and accounted for 66.8% of the total variance. Cronbach's alphas of all 13 items was .839 with the four factor's alphas ranging from .550 to .831. Because the four factors varied in number of items, mean scores were computed for each of the four factors. Pearson's correlation coefficients among the four factors revealed moderately positive correlations among factors, $p \leq$ .001. Taken together, the analyses revealed that the four factors are internally consistent and distinct, independent constructs. Based on this information and to ensure these items corresponded to the first two factors, as well as, ensure the instrument was sufficient enough to answer this study's research questions, the PoPES items were increased by 6 from the original 14 to 20 total questions for the primary study in an effort to ensure solid reliability of coefficients.

Generalized Self-efficacy. To confirm the reliability and validity of the Generalized Self-Efficacy Scale, a confirmatory factor analysis for a one-factor solution was conducted. The results indicated that all items accounted for 48.6% of the total variance. All factor loadings exceeded .350. In addition, the Cronbach's alpha was

.877, demonstrating that all 10 items were internally consistent.

Primary Study, Data Cleaning & Screening

Data was collected for the primary study in the same manner as the pilot study. There were a total of 490 participants who responded to the survey. Of the 490 participants who began the survey, several did not meet the inclusion criteria outlined in Chapter 3. Other participants were removed after checks for invalid cases criteria, as well as, checks for junk text entered in the open field items of the survey (i.e., the AUT required participants to provide six uses for one specific item in the survey). Six participants were removed for that reason. The final N of the study was 286; thus, a 12% invalid rate.

Descriptive Statistics

A summary of the sample descriptive statistics is outlined in Table 6. As shown, the sample had slightly more males than females, and the majority of the sample identified as being White/Caucasian. Over one third of the sample reported having earned a four-year college degree. Just over 20% of the participants reported part-time employment, with the remaining reporting full-time employment. In Table 6, 79% of the participants were either employed full or part time and were in the population of interest for this study.

Table 6

Descriptive Statistics: Categorical Measures

Measure	N	%
Gender		
Male	151	52.80
Female	135	47.20
Total	286	100.00
Race		
American Indian/Native American	5	1.75
Asian	15	5.24
Black/African American	23	8.04
Hispanic/Latino	12	4.20
White/Caucasian	226	79.02
Pacific Islander	2	0.70
Other (please specify)	3	1.05
Total	286	100.00
Race Other		
Mixed Race	2	100.00
Total	2	100.00
Highest Level of Education		
Elementary school only	0	0.00
Some high school, but did not finish	6	2.10
Completed high school	33	11.54
Some college, but did not finish	47	16.43
Two-year college degree	40	13.99
Four-year college degree	105	36.71
Some graduate work	11	3.85
Masters or professional degree	35	12.24
Advanced Graduate work or Ph.D.	9	3.15
Total	286	100.00
Current Employment Status		
Full-Time	225	78.67
Part-Time	61	21.33
Total	286	100.00

Assumptions Testing

Prior to conducting the primary, multivariate analyses, preliminary data screening was conducted to assess the quality of the obtained data and to confirm the assumptions of primary analyses. As previously discussed, invalid cases were removed from the data file, resulting in a final sample size of 286. Given the complexity of the final model, there was insufficient sample to test the theorized model using CB-SEM; as such, the main hypotheses were tested using PLS- SEM in SmartPLS v. 3.0.

Individual indicators, as well as, composite scores were assessed for normality. Normality was examined by evaluation of the skewness, kurtosis, and the mean to standard deviation ratio. Formal tests of normality, such as the Komogrov-Smirnov, were not conducted as these tests have a lower tolerance for deviations from normality than PLS-SEM analytic approaches. Examination of normality indicated that there were no significant violations of normality. Furthermore, there were no concerns with multicollinearity observed.

Model Specification and Quality Assessment

The process of evaluating the overall model consisted of three stages. The first stage of analysis consisted of assessing the measurement quality and ensuring appropriate psychometric properties of the items chosen. Next, the relative weights were calculated using a path weighting scheme and a maximum of 300 iterations. Significance of these paths were assessed by the bootstrapping of 500 samples with no sign changes. Weak and non-significant paths were removed to increase the parsimony of the final model. Furthermore, the evaluation of the quality of the model is assessed through examination of paths, significance, and the measurement quality, which was the processed done for the purposes of this analysis. Effect size and magnitudes of the final model were assessed through the path coefficients as well as the observed R^2 values. Path coefficients are interpreted as follows: $|\sim.10|$ indicates a small effect, $|\sim.30|$ indicates a moderate effect, and $|>.50|$ indicates a large effect. SmartPLS also produces the Standardized Root Mean Square Residual (SRMR) as an indicator of fit. Adequate fit was determined using the recommendation of Hu and Bentler (1999) with a maximum SRMR value of .800.

Key latent constructs were defined as described in Chapter 3. In order to avoid having two indicator constructs, which may create problems in the overall model, composite scores were used for each of the personality dimensions.

Post Hoc PoPES Analysis

The PoPES scale was originally hypothesized to be unidirectional, with one end of the scale representing an open, unstructured problem environment, and the other end a closed, structured environment. The scale items were constructed with this continuum in mind. Some items were intended to represent an open environment (e.g., "Problems can be solved using imagination") and others a closed environment ("Problems can be solved with certain protocols."). Since the scale was theorized to be unidirectional, it was expected that the responses to the "Open" items would be negatively correlated with those of the "Closed" items, as an environment that was more open would tend to be less closed, and vice versa. However, negative correlations were not observed (See Table 10 below).

Prior to testing the theorized model, the measurement model was examined to ensure the quality of the measurement model. Weak (< .500) and non-significant ($p > .05$) indicators were removed from the model to ensure parsimony of the final model. Outer loadings of the final measurement model are outlined below in Table 7.

Table 7

Outer Loadings of Final Measurement Model

Convergent Thinking	Career Commitment	Career Self-Efficacy	Perception of the Problem Environment	Divergent Thinking
AUTBcat	.956			
AUTAcat	.900			
AUTCcat	.897			
CCM1		.877		
CCM2		.884		
CCM4		.880		
CCM10		.781		
GSES1			.733	
GSES10			.727	
GSES2			.715	
GSES3			.551	
GSES4			.721	
GSES5			.729	
GSES6			.767	
GSES7			.764	
GSES8			.689	
GSES9			.701	

POPES1	.751	
POPES10	.592	
POPES14	.766	
POPES15	.753	
POPES16	.795	
POPES17	.769	
POPES18	.702	
POPES19	.722	
POPES20	.805	
POPES3	.739	
POPES4	.783	
POPES6	.692	
RAT1		.688
RAT10		.764
RAT2		.805
RAT3		.673
RAT4		.759
RAT5		.791
RAT6		.597
RAT7		.778
RAT8		.792
RAT9		.832

Note. All coefficients significant, ps < .05

Internal Reliability and Validity Analysis

In order to evaluate the reliability and validity of the measurement mode, the average variance extracted (AVE), composite reliability (CR), and internal consistency (expressed as Cronbach's α) were evaluated based on the recommendations of Fornell and Larcker (1981), Nunally and Bernstien (1994), and Awang (2012); see Table 8. As shown, composite reliabilities for 10 of the 11 constructs were above the critical threshold (.700). Furthermore, the average variance extracted for multiple indicator constructs was above the critical threshold (.500) for all but one latent construct. For both these indicators of model quality, the PoPES Open Environment scale failed to meet the minimally acceptable limits. However, these scores were retained in the model to assess the key hypotheses.

Latent correlations are also shown in Table 8. There was no major indication of multicollinearity or redundancy in the model, evidenced by correlation values under .850. The highest correlation observed was between PoPES Open and PoPES Closed scores (-.835), which would be expected given the fact that these are opposite subscales of the same overall measure. The overall evaluation of the quality of the measurement model suggests adequate reliability and validity.

Table 8

Reliability, Validity, and Latent Correlations

		α	CR	AVE	1	2	3	4	5	6	7	8	9	10
1	Career Commitment	.879	.917	.734										
2	Career Self-Efficacy	.891	.911	.057	.495									
3	Agreeableness				.100	.082	-.008							
4	Conscientiousness				-.139	-.370	-.043	-.335						
5	Convergent Thinking	.907	.942	.843	.020	.124	.071	.150	-.237					
6	Divergent Thinking	.919	.928	.564	-.030	.111	.124	-.006	-.165	.184				
7	Extroversion				-.247	-.157	.040	-.165	.248	-.017	.020			
8	Neuroticism				.164	.351	.081	.256	-.362	.045	.095	-.317		
9	Openness				-.168	-.141	-.088	-.068	.179	-.113	-.037	.198	-.119	
10	Problem Environment	.920	.931	.533	.473	.607	-.205	.023	-.121	-.069	.020	-.081	.141	-.027

Note: AVE = Average Variance Extracted; CR = Composite Reliability

Discriminant validity was assessed by examining the Fornell-Larcker Criterion. Across all measures the Average Variance Extracted within a latent variable was greater than the cross loading to other latent variables, indicating sufficient discriminant validity. Furthermore, observed cross-loadings were highest within each factor, providing further evidence for sufficient discriminant validity. Lastly, multicollinearity was assessed by examining the VIF across latent constructs. Across all constructs, VIF values were < 1.300, indicating a lack of multicollinearity.

Structural Equation Model

Following evaluation of the measurement model, the full conceptual model was examined. Initial assessment of the full theorized model yielded inadequate fit (SRMR = .083). In order to improve model fit and to create the most parsimonious model, nonsignificant paths were removed, resulting in the final model; see Figures 4 and 5. The revised model in Figure 5 had adequate fit with the obtained data, SRMR=.076 and all paths were significant.

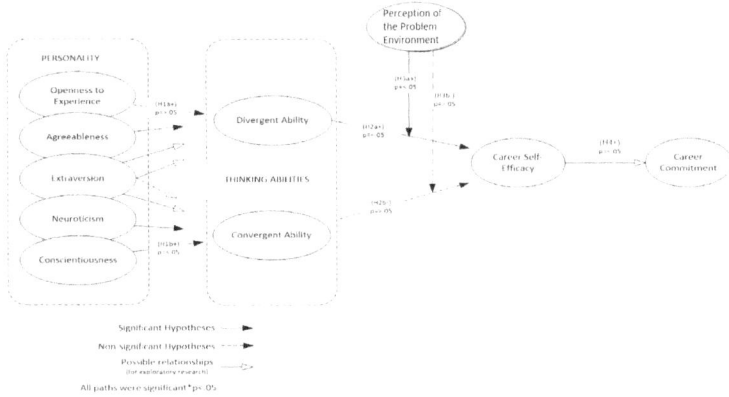

Figure 4. Revised path diagram of associations between personality and CC.

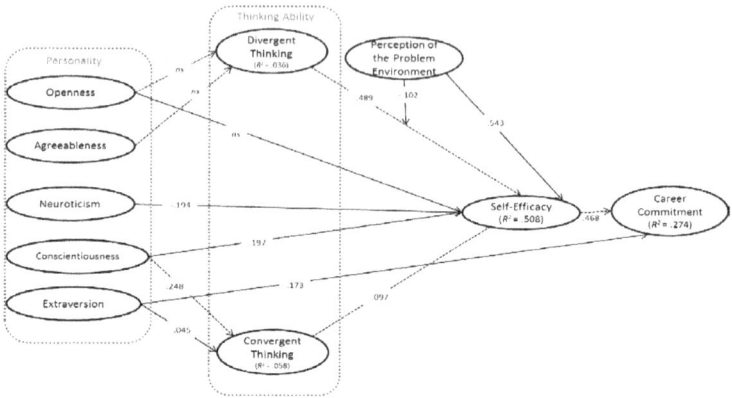

Note. ns = p > .05; all shown paths significant (p < .05).

Figure 5. Summary of the Final Structural Model

Hypothesis Testing Results

H1a. The first hypothesis predicted that openness to experience would be positively associated with Divergent Thinking Abilities. Results from this study failed to provide support for this hypothesis. The pathway between openness to experience on divergent thinking ability was not significant; furthermore, the overall quality and fit of the structural model improved once the path from openness to experience on divergent thinking ability was removed.

H1b. This hypothesis predicted that Conscientiousness would be positively correlated with convergent thinking ability. The path between conscientiousness on convergent thinking ability was significant and positive (.248, p < .05). Higher levels of conscientiousness were associated with higher levels of convergent thinking ability. These results provided full support for this hypothesis.

H2a. This hypothesis predicted that divergent thinking ability would be positively correlated with CSE, which was confirmed by the data (.489, $p < .05$). Higher levels of divergent thinking ability were associated with a higher CSE. The observed relationship was fairly large in magnitude.

H_{2b}. This hypothesis predicted that convergent thinking ability would be positively correlated with CSE. The path between convergent thinking ability on CSE was not significant. Thus, the data failed to support this hypothesis.

H_3. This hypothesis predicted that open problem environment will negatively moderate the association between divergent thinking ability and CSE. The moderating effect of open problem environment and CSE through problem environment was negative and significant (-.102, $p < .05$); thus, providing support for this hypothesis. These results suggest that the relationship between Divergent Thinking Ability and Self-Efficacy varies depending on the level of the problem environment.

H_4. The final hypothesis stated that CSE would be positively correlated with CC. The path between CSE and CC was significant and positive (.468, $p < .05$), thus providing full support for this hypothesis. A summary of the hypothesis testing is outlined below in Table 9.

Additional Findings. The overall model accounted for 50.8 percent of the variance in CSE, and 27.4 % of the variance in CC. Observed effect sizes, expressed as R^2, were relatively low for both Thinking Ability measures. In addition to the hypotheses tested above, the final model found additional significant paths. CSE was positively predicted by openness to experience and conscientiousness, and negatively predicted by neuroticism. Higher levels of extraversion were negatively associated to convergent thinking ability. None of the latent variables were significant predictors of the perception of the problem environment. Furthermore, the interaction of Divergent and Convergent thinking styles was assessed on the perception of the problem environment scores, which further yielded a non-significant relationship. These results indicate that there is not a moderating relationship between Divergent and Convergent thinking on the perception of the problem environment.

In Table 9, Summary of Hypotheses Testing findings, the PLS-SEM models, the bootstrapping estimates a t score, and this is used to determine the significance. A t value greater than 1.96 is significant at the .05 level. However, anything smaller than that is not significant (ns*), p > .05, but the actual p value is not actually calculated.

Table 9

Summary of Hypotheses Testing

Research Question		Hypothesis	Findings
RQ 1: How does personality, in conjunction with the problem environment that characterizes a career, affect a person's commitment to that career?	H1a	Openness to Experience is positively correlated with divergent thinking ability.	*ns
	H1b	Conscientiousness is positively correlated with convergent thinking ability.	.248, $p < .05$
RQ 2: How is personality correlated with specific thinking abilities?	H2a	Divergent thinking ability is positively correlated with CSE.	.097, $p < .05$
	H2b	Convergent thinking ability is positively correlate with CSE.	.489, $p < .05$

RQ 3: How does a person's perception of the career environment interact with their problem-solving abilities, to produce an estimate of CC?	H3	Perception of the Problem Environment scores will be significantly associated with Self-Efficacy.	.543, $p < .05$
RQ 4: How is CSE related to CC?	H4	CSE is positively correlated with CC.	.468, $p < .05$

Table 10

Correlations Among PoPES Items

	1	2	3	4	5	6	7	8	9	10	11	12	13	14	15	16	17	18	19
1																			
2	.295																		
3	.656	.255																	
4	.510	.365	.502																
5	.332	.240	.318	.393															
6	.444	.397	.451	.576	.301														
7	.281	.468	.354	.455	.349	.460													
8	.455	.216	.410	.385	.392	.461	.398												
9	.114	.347	.119	.150	.462	.135	.170	.291											
10	.229	0.041	.283	.208	.340	.183	0.021	.226	.534										
11	.196	.147*	.242	.512	.469	.358	.326	.360	.294	.378									
12	.222	.483	.260	.535	.272	.447	.427	.329	.281	.240	.542								
13	.277	.370	.314	.459	.370	.433	.463	.343	.294	.260	.528	.662							
14	.462	.160	.454	.577	.336	.508	.331	.418	.130*	.390	.479	.427	.512						
15	.472	.370	.512	.707	.338	.577	.499	.383	.040	0.061	.400	.485	.428	.539					
16	.535	.128	.538	.563	.415	.425	.351	.530	.167	.343	.408	.288	.291	.553	.572				
17	.551	.188	.519	.470	.395	.380	.349	.493	.232	.337	.397	.300	.314	.532	.442	.750			
18	.541	.192	.454	.391	.373	.333	.241	.469	.323	.435	.328	.277	.380	.542	.319	.538	.619		
19	.493	.281	.455	.492	.463	.387	.300	.430	.315	.419	.413	.383	.400	.513	.397	.527	.613	.689	
20	.539	.194	.545	.514	.402	.438	.304	.477	.202	.415	.399	.352	.447	.628	.461	.641	.682	.704	.726

These results suggest that all items of the newly developed tool appeared to measure the perception of the problem environment in a unidirectional way. To further explore this, a principle component analysis (PCA) was conducted forcing all items to one factor. The results indicated that the set of items accounted for 43.33% of the variance. A summary of the factor loadings of all 20 items are outlined below in Table 11.

Table 11

Factor Loadings for PoPES Items Forced to One Factor

Factor Loading	
...can be solved using known rules	.675
...can be solved using imagination	
...can be solved using established procedures	.676
...require careful, detailed thinking	.761
...require lots of cooperation from outside groups	.595
...require keeping the goal clearly in sight	.670
...require flexibility to deal with changing requirements	.569
...rely on rules of thumb	.651
...usually require cutting corners	
...have only one "best" solution	
...are very complex	.620
...require innovative thinking	.615
...require many skills, if they are to be solved satisfactorily	.644
...require a systematic approach	.746
...require decision-making	.705
...can be solved using known policies and directives	.756
...can be solved using current regulations	.752
...require following a pre-made plan	.713
...involve completing existing checklists	.753
...can be solved with certain protocols	.793

Note. Factor loadings < .500 are suppressed

These results continued to support the notion that perception of the problem environment was a unidirectional construct. The 20-item PoPES scales was theorized to be broken down in the following Open and Closed items in Table 12:

Table 12

Item	Closed	Item	Open
1	...can be solved using known rules	2	...can be solved using imagination
3	...can be solved using established procedures	5	...require lots of cooperation from outside groups
4	...require careful, detailed thinking	7	...require flexibility to deal with changing requirements
6	...require keeping the goal clearly in sight	9	...usually require cutting corners
8	...rely on rules of thumb	12	...require innovative thinking
10	...have only one "best" solution	13	...require many skills, if they are to be solved satisfactorily
11	...are very complex	15	...require decision-making
14	...require a systematic approach	19	...involve completing existing checklists
16	...can be solved using known policies and directives	20	...can be solved with certain protocols
17	regulations		
18	...require following a pre-made plan		

To examine these relationships, sum scores were computed for Open and Closed items based on the theorized classification. There was not a significant difference between these scores ($p = .249$), providing further support that the scores could not be classified by Open and Closed categories. More research may be needed to further investigate the complexity of Problem Environments.

Summary

This chapter outlined the analytic process and statistical findings of this study. The results of the study continue to build on the prior knowledge by linking key personality factors to career commitment through career self-efficacy. Examination of the newly- developed PoPES tool indicated that further research may be needed to further understand the Perception of the problem environment concept and its complexity, and this complexity may be within the problem itself or a cognitive complexity. The following chapter will discuss the theoretical and conceptual explanation of these and other findings. Additionally, it will discuss implication for policy, practice, and future research.

CHAPTER 5

DISCUSSION, IMPLICATIONS & CONCLUSION

Discussion, Implications, and Conclusion

In this chapter, the results of this study, focusing upon hypothesis testing, are summarized and discussed in relation to previous literature, along with limitations of the current study and possibilities for future research. A number of limitations as well as possibilities for future research are presented and discussed, followed by the study's conclusion.

The purpose of this research was to construct and evaluate a statistical model linking personality traits to CC, connect empirical and theoretical frameworks that drive the primary and ancillary research questions and hypotheses, and relate personality traits and CC through the moderation of an individual's perception of problem solving in the career environment as mediated by CSE. As stated previously, no past research has established a theoretical link between personality traits and CC, in the context of the types of problems that characterize work in a career from an interactional perspective. This study attempted to fill the literature gap by examining one primary research question and four ancillary ones as outline in Chapter 2. The main and primary research question attempted to fill the gap in literature by exploring the relationship and theoretical link between personality and CC as characterized by the perception of the problem environment. Further, this research was designed to explore personality traits and how they link to the workplace which contributes to the empirical expansion of previous meta-analytic studies that had solely focused on an individual's personality dimensions and their performance. To investigate the relationships among the variables, PLS-SEM, was used to explore the dynamic complexities between the cause and effect relationships, as well as, explain variance in the data collected and presented in the final research model at Figure 4 (Hair et al., 2010).

This study tested four hypotheses utilizing a varied group of participants from various educational backgrounds, careers, and socioeconomic backgrounds to break down the broad and multi-dimensional aspects of each of the variables. I will explore the results and outcome summary of each in the next section.

Results and Outcome Summary

H$_{1a}$: Openness to Experience is positively correlated with Divergent Thinking Ability.

The findings of this study revealed that Openness to Experience was not significantly associated with divergent or convergent thinking abilities. This is in general opposition to the findings in extant literature (Barrick & Mount, 2005; Chamorro-Premuzic & Reichenbacher, 2008; George & Zhou, 2001; LePine, Colquitt, & Erez, 2000; King et al., 1996; McCrae, 1987). It can therefore be surmised that while this personality trait may not be directly associated with an individual's cognitive abilities; it may serve as more of a predictor of an individual's willingness to express themselves and explore alternate solutions to solve problems (Batey, Chamorro-Premuzic, and Furnham, 2010).

H$_{1b}$: Consciousness is positively correlated with Convergent Thinking Ability

The results corresponded with some previous findings that suggested that highly conscientious individuals may have difficulties with open problems that require divergent thinking abilities, but they may be more suited to solve closed problems that require convergent thinking abilities (Le et al., 2011), but not others (Chamorro-Premuzic & Furnham, 2005) who asserted that conscientiousness is not related to divergent thinking abilities which suggests, albeit weakly, that if it is related to thinking ability in any way, then it is related to the other end of the spectrum, which is convergent thinking ability. The results of the study illustrated that conscientiousness is a strong predictor of convergent thinking abilities.

H$_{2a}$: Divergent thinking ability is positively correlated with CSE

The results from this study found that divergent thinking ability was related to CSE which is consistent with the prior research of (Beghetto, 2006; Choi, 2004; Gomez-Mejia et al., 2007; Guilford, 1967; Jaussi, Randel, & Dionne, 2007; Lim & Choi, 2009; Tierney & Farmer, 2010). These findings continue to support the exploration of creativity as a proxy of divergent thinking abilities and CSE.

H$_{2b}$: Convergent thinking is positively correlated with CSE.

However, Hypothesis 2b, which posited a positive relationship between convergent thinking abilities and CSE, did not achieve significance. The findings did not support the basis of the results and convergent thinking abilities was not significantly associated with CSE. This conflicts with previous literature (Marziano & Hefleblower, 2011) who suggested that the ability to select the best course of action through convergent thinking may result in higher CSE.

H$_3$: An open problem environment negatively moderates the association between divergent thinking ability and CSE and H$_{3b}$: A closed problem environment will positively moderate the association between convergent thinking ability and CSE.

The results of the study found that an open environment was a significant, negative moderator on the relationship between divergent thinking abilities and CSE. These findings continue to support the use of the General Systems Theory in practice. This will allow for the exploration of an individual's interaction with an open problem environment and how the boundaries of the environment influence that interaction. The findings were consistent with the prior research of Malik (2013).

Conversely, the results of the study failed to indicate significant moderation with respect to the effect of a closed problem environment moderating the association between convergent thinking ability and CSE, failing to support Hypotheses 3b. The results conflict with extant literature (Colzato, Szapora, Lippelt & Hommel, n.d.; Kwon, Park, and Park, 2006; Malik, 2013). The results of the study did not support that the perception of the problem environment, as defined by a closed problem, influenced the strength of the relationship between the convergent thinking abilities and CSE. The intent was not to categorize the perception of the problem environment in some absolute sense but to attempt to predict individual behavior. This directly supports the continuance to explore this unexamined novel phenomenon that seeks to examine how personality dimensions are related to workplace behavior.

H$_4$: CSE is positively correlated with CC.

Finally, with respect to Hypothesis 4, a significant result was found. A significant, positive association was indicated between CSE and CC. In extant literature, (Beghetto, 2006; Cervone & Peake, 1986; Choi, 2004; Jaussi et al., 2007; Karwowski et al., 2010; Lim & Choi, 2009; Tierney & Farmer, 2002, 2010) found that CC is correlated with individual and organizational performance, self-efficacy, and job satisfaction. The structural equation model showed that CSE was highly related to CC. In other words, individuals with higher CSE exhibited increased

CC. Conversely, individuals with lower CSE demonstrated lower levels of CC.

Implications to Theory

This study has both theoretical and practical implications. The results of this study found similarities with extant literature that explained CC on the basis of personality differences (Aluja & Garcia, 2004), as well as, behavioral consequences (Podsakoff, Bommer, Podsakoff, & MacKenzie, 2006), and this study served to expand this area of research by examining the relationship between personality and CC through an interactional perspective. While not all hypotheses were supported, a relationship between personality traits and CC was definitively determined on the basis of the analyses conducted. Also, theoretically, this is the first study to contribute the PoPES scale which was developed and inducted into this study because the perception of the problem environment is an unfamiliar phenomenon and little theory exists on it. This scale serves as a start point for researchers and practitioners to further investigate individual behaviors and their propensity to solve problems. Managers can utilize this information to connect employees with the best career that fits their personality trait, their approach to solving problems based on their thinking abilities, as well as, their perception of the environment. The results of the study substantiate the need for additional exploration of the theoretical proposition of the instrument given the novelty of it. Future researchers may attempt replication of this instrument to increase confidence in its use amongst academic and practitioners. This will help to improve the scales reliability and usability in future studies and enhance the future of the organizational behavior field of study.

The results of this study highlighted the importance and relevance of personality traits, corresponding with previous literature and theory (Aluja & Garcia, 2004; Chamorro-Premuzic & Reichenbacher, 2008; Cloninger et al., 1993; Matthews, Deary, & Whiteman, 2003).

Specifically, the five factor model was found to be relevant and important in the context of prediction (De Fruyt, McCrae, Szirmak, & Nagy, 2004; Gurven, von Rueden, Massenkoff,

Kaplan, & Vie, 2013; McCrae & John, 1992; McCrae & Costa, 2008; O'Connor, 2002; Tupes & Christal, 1992). Important differences between convergent and divergent thinking were also found (Guildford, 1983), while links between personality traits and thinking abilities were also indicated (McCrae, 1987). Also, the relationship between CSE and CC was found to be positive in this study, which aligns with previous literature (Artino, LaRochelle, & Durning, 2010, Prat-Sala & Redford, 2010; Sawatzky, Ratner, Richardson, Washburn, Sudmant, & Mirwaldt, 2012).

Practical Implications of the Research

There are several implications for both researchers of personality traits and agencies that seek to determine how to remain competitive and attract and maintain individuals committed to their career. The first implication is that organizations need to continue to explore individual employee's thinking abilities by utilizing career assessment tools and executing employee surveys and assessment tools, and investigating how individual's approach their perception of the problem environment through interactions with other people, tools, or systems they may use to solve problems. Organizations may also evaluate their employee's self-efficacy which may or may not influence their commitment to an organization. This increased scrutiny of an individual's behavior can inform an organization's perspective on the nature of the environment they provide their employees, as well as, explain how an individual's perception of that environment impacts extent to which their thinking abilities and interactions interplay with their personality and CC.

The second implication is that this study informed the TRA based on an individual's intent to perform a job task or perform a behavior may be conditioned by more than an individual's CC but rather an individual's global view of their perception of the problem environment and their own self-efficacy which also have effects on whether they commit to a particular career or not. An individual's commitment to their career is largely driven by their belief that they can and will be successful. Adapting the PoPES, a new instrument and means to measure an individual's perception of their problem environment, which could lead to indicators that mitigate less than favorable sustainability of an organization's competitive edge due to lack of an individual's commitment to a career or job.

Thirdly, while significant research has been undertaken to examine the theoretical link between personality and CC; little to no research has been undertaken to measure and improve an individual's perception of the problem environment. Therefore, it is critical that organizations and researchers identify and conduct analyses of individuals, not just those who work autonomously but those who work in multi-faceted and multi-disciplined teams, to determine the core principles and means to motivate and retain them during complex, turbulent, uncertain, and ambiguous conditions and situations. This research and the PoPES instrument may be used for employers; more likely, to be used for self-analysis and counseling. Further, organizations may use it but considering the legal strictures, it may be more worthwhile for self-analysis.

This research study has the potential to influence to which an individual's propensity to solve problems and how that may prove useful to organizations as they design policies and procedures to improve the quality of their selection and hiring of the best fit of personnel to their organization.

Doing so, may reduce less favorable perceptions and build stronger commitments to careers.

Limitations of the Research & Recommendations for Future Direction

A number of limitations were present within the study. First, the small sample size used for these analyses constituted the largest limitation present within this study. The final sample size, which consisted of under 300 respondents, necessitated the use of partial least squares in the context of structural equation modeling, with this specific methodology incorporating a number of limitations and drawbacks. However, this methodology was deemed necessary due to the sample size obtained.

Additionally, this study used cross-sectional data in its analysis. With the use of cross-sectional data as opposed to panel data, causality cannot be determined with respect to any analyses conducted. Additionally, the low internal consistency reliability associated with the BFI items also constituted a limitation of this study. Among all five subscales, internal consistency reliability was found to be low based on the Cronbach's alpha values found.

While the use of this scale was not deemed to constitute a limitation of the current study, a future study potentially incorporating the full 44-item inventory would hopefully achieve acceptable levels of reliability with respect to these items.

Another limitation was that the survey was limited to the survey questions within the study from the seven instruments and collected at a single point in time. Further, it was assumed that all participants would be truthful in their responses to the survey questions, and as noted above in both the pilot and primary study findings, that was not the case in several instances. Further, it is unknown whether the incorporation of demographic characteristics impacted or camouflaged the real variances in the findings.

Another limitation of this study consisted of administering this survey at a single point in time. This results in cross-sectional data, which cannot be used to definitively determine causality between measures. With respect to future research conducted, it is recommended that the administration of the survey be conducted over time with the same respondents to gather panel data, which can be used to determine causality, ideally on a nationally representative sample of respondents.

Conclusion

This study provided a number of important contributions to current research and theory within this area of study. Many discrepancies were found between this current study's findings and that of previous literature, which opens up the possibility for a large body of future research which could explore the relationships between these concepts in further detail in an effort to rectify these discrepancies. A large set of important new findings came out of the present study, along with contributions to theory. While this study contained several limitations, these limitations can be overcome in future research.

This study was largely theory driven, underpinned by the TRA, and it was highly exploratory in nature to allow for the investigation of the effects of personality traits on CC, in the context of the problem solving environment. The main and original contribution to the Organizational Behavior (OB) field of study was the PoPES scale. This measurement instrument explored the moderating effects of an individual's perception of the problem environment on CC. Managers who quickly identify the necessity for change, improve processes, and implement emergent technologies and tools that improve an individual's perception of their environment, increase support and CC. Managers who leverage the value of knowing their employee's behavioral intent and what motivates them will enhance their ability to match people with careers that they believe they will be successful in which will increase their commitment to a job, task, or career.

Additional future research direction is to: 1) administer the survey over time with the same respondents to gather panel data, which can be used to determine causality, ideally on a nationally representative sample of respondents, 2) attempt to replicate the PoPES instrument to understand what exactly it is measuring and to increase confidence in its use amongst academic and practitioners, and 3) continue exploring the problem solving environment from an interactional perspective to further investigate how people create meaning during interactions in different complex problem environments.

APPENDIX A (Pilot Study Consent Form): CONSENT TO PARTICIPATE IN RESEARCH

"Do Job-Specific Problems and Individual Problem-Solving Abilities Mediate the Relationship Between Personality and Career Commitment? An Empirical Investigation."

CONSENT TO PARTICIPATE IN RESEARCH

You are asked to participate in a research study conducted by Crystal Washington, doctoral candidate, from the College of Business Administration at Trident University International. The results of the proposed study will contribute to completion of a dissertation.

You are eligible to participate is you are 18 years of age or older, can understand English and read at the 5th grade level, are a US citizen located in the US, and are currently employed.

PURPOSE OF THE STUDY

The purpose of this pilot study will be to validate the instruments, Perception of the Problem Environment Scale (PoPES) and modified General Self-Efficacy (GSE) instruments, before they are included in the primary study.

PROCEDURES

In the pilot study, approximately 120 participants will be asked to complete the PoPES and GSE instruments. You will also have to answer a few questions about yourself to confirm that you are eligible to participate. The study site location is an online website. If you agree to participate in this project, please answer the questions on the questionnaire as best you can. It should take approximately 5-10 minutes to complete. Please review your answers and click submit to respond to the survey.

CONFIDENTIALITY

Data downloaded from PsychData will include a unique respondent ID that is used by the online tool to verify your participation. However, this unique respondent ID number is not connected to any information that can be linked to your identity. Your information is completely anonymous, and no participant identifiers will be stored. Any information that is obtained in connection with this study and that can be identified with you will remain confidential and will be disclosed only with your permission or as required by law.

POTENTIAL RISKS AND DISCOMFORTS

The study involves no foreseeable risks or harm to you. The risks associated with this study are minimal and are not greater than risks ordinarily encountered in daily life.

POTENTIAL BENEFITS TO SUBJECTS AND/OR TO SOCIETY

There is not benefit to the participant. There will be no financial benefit from participation in the survey provided by the Principal Investigator. The proposed study advances the field of organizational behavior by applying personality traits to the study of career commitment. It assists in the hiring and selecting personnel. It provides employees with a self-assessment tool to better understand their view of open and closed problems, which can be used to determine their commitment to a particular career. It also affords managers with an opportunity to understand the fit or lack of fit between their employees' thinking abilities and perception of the problem-solving environments to deter a lack of career commitment. Operationalization of the proposed surveys may lead to future studies.

PAYMENT FOR PARTICIPATION

If you are eligible to participate in this study, you will earn points for participation according to the Panel Rewards Terms and Conditions approved by Survey Sampling International, LLC ("SSI"). These points will be credited to your panelist account by SSI at the conclusion of the study. Your participation is strictly voluntary.

PARTICIPATION AND WITHDRAWAL

You can choose whether to be in this study or not. If you volunteer to be in this study, you may withdraw at any time without consequences of any kind. Participation or non- participation will not affect you or any other personal consideration or right you usually expect. You may also refuse to answer any questions you don't want to answer and still remain in the study. The investigator may withdraw you from this research if circumstances arise that in the opinion of the researcher warrant doing so.

IDENTIFICATION OF INVESTIGATORS

If you have any questions or concerns about the research, please feel free to contact, Crystal Washington, Doctoral Candidate and Principal Investigator, via email at crystal.washington@my.trident.edu, (800) 375-9878, with Trident University International (TUI). Dr. Roger Rensvold, Faculty lead – College of Business Administration and

Crystal's Dissertation Chairperson, can be reached at roger.rensvold@trident.edu, Telephone: (800) 375-9878 ext. 2327.

RIGHTS OF RESEARCH SUBJECTS

You may withdraw your consent at any time and discontinue participation without penalty. You are not waiving any legal claims, rights or remedies because of your participation in this research study. If you have questions regarding your rights as a research subject, contact the Institutional Review Board for the Protection of Human Subjects at Trident University International, 5757 Plaza Drive, Suite 100, Cypress, California 90630; Telephone: (714) 226-9840; Email: IRB@trident.edu.

During this study, if the researchers discover any new information that might cause you to change your mind about participating, the researchers will share this new information with you.

SIGNATURE OF RESEARCH SUBJECT OR LEGAL REPRESENTATIVE

I understand the procedures and conditions of my participation described above. My questions have been answered to my satisfaction, and I agree to participate in this study. I have been given a copy of this form.

*

I have read the informed consent information above and (choose one):

○ I agree to participate

○ I do not agree to participate

Do you understand the English language?

Yes

No

Can you read at or above the 5th grade reading level?

Yes

No

What is your age?

Under 18 years

18 to 25 years

26 to 39 years

40 to 64 years

65 years or older

Are you currently employed?

Yes

No

Are you a US citizen?

Yes

No

Which state do you currently reside?

-Select-

Other:

PROPOSED PERCEPTION of the PROBLEM ENVIRONMENT SCALE (PoPES)

In my line of work, the problems I encounter on the job ....

	Strongly Disagree	Disagree	Tend to Disagree	Tend to Agree	Agree	Strongly Agree
...can be solved using known rules	O	O	O	O	O	O
...can be solved using imagination	O	O	O	O	O	O
...can be solved using established procedures	O	O	O	O	O	O
...require careful, detailed thinking	O	O	O	O	O	O
...require lots of cooperation from outside groups	O	O	O	O	O	O
...require keeping the goal clearly in sight	O	O	O	O	O	O
...require flexibility to deal with changing requirements	O	O	O	O	O	O
...rely on rules of thumb	O	O	O	O	O	O
...usually require cutting corners	O	O	O	O	O	O
...have only one "best" solution	O	O	O	O	O	O
...are very complex	O	O	O	O	O	O
...require innovative thinking	O	O	O	O	O	O
...require many skills, if they are to be solved satisfactorily	O	O	O	O	O	O

...require a systematic approach	○	○	○
...require decision-making	○	○	○
...can be solved using known policies and directives	○	○	○
...can be solved using current regulations	○	○	○
...require following a pre-made plan	○	○	○
...involve completing existing checklists	○	○	○
...can be solved with certain protocols	○	○	○

(Modified) GENERALIZED SELF-EFFICACY SCALE

In this section, we will assess the strength of your individual belief in your own ability to respond to novel or difficult situations and to deal with any associated obstacles or setbacks. What is the strength of your individual belief in your own ability to respond to novel or difficult situations and to deal with any associated obstacles or setbacks?

Rating Scale: 1 = Not at all true 2 = Hardly true 3 = Moderately true 4 = Exactly true

1. I can quickly organize my thoughts to solve difficult problems.
2. I can perform well and commit to mastering a challenge.

3. If someone opposes me, I can find the means and ways to get what I want.
4. I can apply critical thinking abilities to accomplish my goals and commit to a career.
5. I am confident that I can deal efficiently with unexpected events and still remain committed to a career.
6. Thanks to my resourcefulness, I can handle unforeseen situations in different environments and still remain committed to a career.
7. I can solve most problems and produce desired outcomes if I invest the necessary effort.
8. I can remain calm and persevere when facing difficulties.
9. When I am confronted with a problem, I can apply my knowledge and skills to find several solutions.
10. If I am in trouble, I can usually think of a solution and act with a strong degree of commitment.

What is your gender?
- Male
- Female
- Transgender or gender variant In what year were you born?

In what year were you born?

| -Select- |

How would you describe your current employment status?

- Employed full time
- Employed part time
- Military/Active Duty
- Unemployed

Thank You!

APPENDIX A (Primary Study Consent Form)
CONSENT TO PARTICIPATE IN RESEARCH

"Do Job-Specific Problems and Individual Problem-Solving Abilities Mediate the Relationship Between Personality and Career Commitment? An Empirical Investigation."

CONSENT TO PARTICIPATE IN RESEARCH

You are asked to participate in a research study conducted by Crystal Washington, doctoral candidate, from the College of Business Administration at Trident University International. The results of the proposed study will contribute to completion of a dissertation.

You are eligible to participate is you are 18 years of age or older, can understand English and read at the 5th grade level, are a US citizen located in the US, and are currently employed.

PURPOSE OF THE STUDY

The purpose of this study is to establish a relationship between personality traits and career commitment, in the context of the types of problems that characterize work in a specific career.

PROCEDURES

In the primary study, approximately 235 participants will be asked to complete the Big Five Instrument (BFI), Remote Associates Test (RAT), Alternate Uses Test (AUT), Perception of the Problem Environment Scale (PoPES), General Self-Efficacy (GSE) Scale, Career Commitment Measure (CCM), and answer a few demographic questions. You will also have to answer a few questions about yourself to confirm that you are eligible to participate. The study site location is an online website. If you agree to participate in this project, please answer the questions on the questionnaire as best you can. It should take approximately 25-30 minutes to complete. Please review your answers and click submit to respond to the survey.

CONFIDENTIALITY

Data downloaded from PsychData will include a unique respondent ID that is used by the online tool to verify your participation. However, this unique respondent ID number is not connected to any information that can be linked to your identity. Your information is completely anonymous and no participant identifiers will be stored. Any information that is obtained in connection with this study and that can be identified with you will remain confidential and will be disclosed only with your permission or as required by law.

POTENTIAL RISKS AND DISCOMFORTS

The study involves no foreseeable risks or harm to you. The risks associated with this study are minimal and are not greater than risks ordinarily encountered in daily life.

POTENTIAL BENEFITS TO SUBJECTS AND/OR TO SOCIETY

There is not benefit to the participant. There will be no financial benefit from participation in the survey provided by the Principal Investigator. The proposed study advances the field of organizational behavior by applying personality traits to the study of career commitment. It assists in the hiring and selecting personnel. It provides employees with a self-assessment tool to better understand their view of open and closed problems, which can be used to determine their commitment to a particular career. It also affords managers with an opportunity to understand the fit or lack of fit between their employees' thinking abilities and perception of the problem-solving environments to deter a lack of career commitment. Operationalization of the proposed surveys may lead to future studies.

PAYMENT FOR PARTICIPATION

If you are eligible to participate in this study, you will earn points for participation according to the Panel Rewards Terms and Conditions approved by Survey Sampling International, LLC ("SSI"). These points will be credited to your panelist account by SSI at the conclusion of the study. Your participation is strictly voluntary.

PARTICIPATION AND WITHDRAWAL

You can choose whether to be in this study or not. If you volunteer to be in this study, you may withdraw at any time without consequences of any kind. Participation or non- participation will not affect you or any other personal consideration or right you usually expect. You may also refuse to answer any questions you don't want to answer and still remain in the study. The investigator may withdraw you from this research if circumstances arise that in the opinion of the researcher warrant doing so.

IDENTIFICATION OF INVESTIGATORS

If you have any questions or concerns about the research, please feel free to contact, Crystal Washington,

Doctoral Candidate and Principal Investigator, via email at crystal.washington@my.trident.edu, (800) 375-9878, with Trident University International (TUI). Dr. Roger Rensvold, Faculty lead – College of Business Administration and Crystal's Dissertation Chairperson, can be reached at roger.rensvold@trident.edu, Telephone: (800) 375-9878 ext. 2327.

RIGHTS OF RESEARCH SUBJECTS

You may withdraw your consent at any time and discontinue participation without penalty. You are not waiving any legal claims, rights or remedies because of your participation in this research study. If you have questions regarding your rights as a research subject, contact the Institutional Review Board for the Protection of Human Subjects at Trident University International, 5757 Plaza Drive, Suite 100, Cypress, California 90630; Telephone: (714) 226-9840; Email: IRB@trident.edu.

During this study, if the researchers discover any new information that might cause you to change your mind about participating, the researchers will share this new information with you.

SIGNATURE OF RESEARCH SUBJECT OR LEGAL REPRESENTATIVE

I understand the procedures and conditions of my participation described above. My questions have been answered to my satisfaction, and I agree to participate in this study. I have been given a copy of this form.

*

I have read the informed consent information above and (choose one):

○ I agree to participate

○ I do not agree to participate

Do you understand the English language?

Yes

No

Can you read at or above the 5th grade reading level?

Yes

No

What is your age?

Under 18 years

18 to 25 years

26 to 39 years

40 to 64 years

65 years or older

Are you currently employed?

Yes

No

Are you a US citizen?

Yes

No

Which state do you currently reside?

[-Select-]

[Other:]

What is your gender?

- Male
- Female
- Transgender or gender variant In what year were you born?

In what year were you born?

[-Select-]

How would you describe your current employment status?

- Employed full time
- Employed part time
- Military/Active Duty
- Unemployed

APPENDIX B: BIG FIVE INSTRUMENT (BFI)

English version.

Instruction: How well do the following statements describe your personality?

I see myselft as someone who...	Disagree strongly	Disagree a little	Neither agree or disagree	Agree a little	Agree strongly
...is reserved	(1)	(2)	(3)	(4)	(5)
...is generally trusting					
...tends to be lazy					
...is relaxed, handles stress well					
...has few artistic interest					
...is outgoing, sociable					
...tends to find fault with others					
...does a thorough job					
...gets nervous easily					
...has an active imagination					

Scoring the BF 1-10 scales:
Extraversion IR.6; Agreeableness: 2, 7R; Conscientiousness: 3R, 8; Neuroticism: 4R, 9; Openness: 5R 10 (R = item is reversed-scored).

APPENDIX C: REMOTE ASSOCATION TEST (RAT)

RP#_____

Version-H

Remote Associates Test

Each of the ten problems below consist of three "clue" words. For each problem, please think of a forth word that relates to each of the other three "clue" words. Weite your response on the line alongside each problem.

Example:
Elephant-Lapse-Vivid   Answer: Memory

1. Bass-Complex-Sleep   _____
2. Chamber-Staff-Box   _____
3. Desert-Ice-Spell   _____
4. Base-Show-Dance   _____
5. Inch-Deal-Peg   _____
6. Soap-Shoe-Tissue   _____
7. Blood-Music-Cheese   _____
8. Skunk-Kings-Boiled   _____
9. Jump-Kill-Bliss   _____
10. Shopping-Washer-Picture   _____

APPENDIX D: ALTERNATE USES TEST (AUT)

In Guilford's Alternative Uses Task (1967) examinees are asked to list as many possible uses for a common house hold item (such as brick, a paperclip, a newspaper).

In this test, you will be asked to consider some common objects. Each object has a common use, which will be stated. You are to list as many as six other uses for which the object or parts of the object could serve:

Example:

Given: A NEWSPAPER (used for reading). You might think of the following other uses for a newspaper.

a. Start a fire
b. Wrap garbage
c. Swat flies
d. Stuffing to pack boxes
e. Line drawers or shelves
f. Make up a kidnap note

Notice that all of the uses listed are different from each other and different form the primary use of a newspaper.

Each acceptable use must be different from others and from the common use.

Scoring is comprised of four components:

1. Originality - each response it compared to the total amount of responses from all of the people you gave the test to. Responses that were given by only 5% of your group are unusual (1 point), responses that were given by only 1% of your

group are unique - 2 points). Total all the point. Higher scores indicate creativity*

2. Fluency - total. Just add up all the responses. In this example it is 6.

3. Flexibility - or different categories. In this case there are five different categories (weapon and hit sister are from the same general idea of weapon)

4. Elaboration - amount of detail (for Example "a doorstop" = 0 whereas "a door stop to prevent a door slamming shut in a strong wind" = 2 (one for explanation of door slamming, two for further detail about the wind).

*There is a contamination problem and can be corrected by using a corrective calculation for originality (originality = originality/fluency).

APPENDIX E: PERCEPTION of the PROBLEM ENVIRONMENT SCALE (PoPES)

Developer: Crystal Washington, PhD Student In my line of work, the problems I encounter on the job ....

	Strongly Disagree	Disagree	Tend to Disagree	Tend to Agree	Agree	Strongly Agree
...can be solved using known rules	O	O	O	O	O	O
...can be solved using imagination	O	O	O	O	O	O
...can be solved using established procedures	O	O	O	O	O	O
...require careful, detailed thinking	O	O	O	O	O	O
...require lots of cooperation from outside groups	O	O	O	O	O	O
...require keeping the goal clearly in sight	O	O	O	O	O	O
...require flexibility to deal with changing requirements	O	O	O	O	O	O
...rely on rules of thumb	O	O	O	O	O	O
...usually require cutting corners	O	O	O	O	O	O
... have only one "best" solution	O	O	O	O	O	O
...are very complex	O	O	O	O	O	O

...require innovative thinking	○	○	○	○	○
...require many skills, if they are to be solved satisfactorily	○	○	○	○	○
...require a systematic approach	○	○	○	○	○
...require decision-making	○	○	○	○	
...can be solved using known policies and directives	○	○	○	○	○
...can be solved using current regulations	○	○	○	○	○
...require following a pre-made plan	○	○	○	○	○
...involve completing existing checklists	○	○	○	○	○
...can be solved with certain protocols	○	○	○	○	○

SCORING INSTRUCTIONS

To score the PoPES, you will need to do the following:

Closed Environment: You have to reverse-score items 2, 5, 7, 8, 9, 11, 12 and 13.

Raw Scores	Recoded Scores
1	6
2	5
3	4
4	3
5	2
6	1

If you do that, only for items 2, 5, 7, 8, 9, 11, 12, and 13 (additional items 15 and 19), then the average score for a "mostly closed" environment is 6. The score for a "mostly open" environment would be 1.

If, on the other hand, you decide that you want a high score on the PoPES scale to indicate an OPEN environment, then you would recode the other items instead: 1, 3, 4, 6, 10, and 14 (additional items 16, 17, 18 and 20).

APPENDIX F: (Modified) GENERALIZED SELF-EFFICACY SCALE

In this section, we will assess the strength of your individual belief in your own ability to respond to novel or difficult situations and to deal with any associated obstacles or setbacks. What is the strength of your individual belief in your own ability to respond to novel or difficult situations and to deal with any associated obstacles or setbacks?

Rating Scale: 1 = Not at all true 2 = Hardly true 3 = Moderately true 4 = Exactly true

1. I can quickly organize my thoughts to solve difficult problems.
2. I can perform well and commit to mastering a challenge.
3. If someone opposes me, I can find the means and ways to get what I want.
4. I can apply critical thinking abilities to accomplish my goals and commit to a career.
5. I am confident that I can deal efficiently with unexpected events and still remain committed to a career.
6. Thanks to my resourcefulness, I can handle unforeseen situations in different environments and still remain committed to a career.
7. I can solve most problems and produce desired outcomes if I invest the necessary effort.

8. I can remain calm and persevere when facing difficulties.
9. When I am confronted with a problem, I can apply my knowledge and skills to find several solutions.
10. If I am in trouble, I can usually think of a solution and act with a strong degree of commitment.

Scoring: Add up all responses to a sum score. The range is from 10 to 40 points.

APPENDIX G: CAREER COMMITMENT MEASURE (CCM)

1. My line of work/career field is an important part of who I am.

   Strongly Disagree | Disagree | Neither Disagree of Agree | Agree | Strongly Agree

2. This line of work/ career field has a great deal of personal meaning to me.

   Strongly Disagree | Disagree | Neither Disagree of Agree | Agree | Strongly Agree

3. I do not feel 'emotionally attached' to this line of work/ career field (R).

   Strongly Disagree | Disagree | Neither Disagree of Agree | Agree | Strongly Agree

4. I strongly identify with my chosen line of work/career field.

   Strongly Disagree | Disagree | Neither Disagree of Agree | Agree | Strongly Agree

5. The costs associated with my line of work/career field sometimes seem too great.

   Strongly Disagree | Disagree | Neither Disagree of Agree | Agree | Strongly Agree

6. Given the problems I encounter in this line of work/career field, I sometimes wonder if I get enough out of it.

| Strongly Disagree | Disagree | Neither Disagree of Agree | Agree | Strongly Agree |

7. Given the problems in this line of work/career field, I sometimes wonder if the personal burden is worth it.

| Strongly Disagree | Disagree | Neither Disagree of Agree | Agree | Strongly Agree |

8. The discomforts associated with my line of work/career field sometimes seem too great.

| Strongly Disagree | Disagree | Neither Disagree of Agree | Agree | Strongly Agree |

9. I do not have a strategy for achieving my goals in this line of work/career field.

| Strongly Disagree | Disagree | Neither Disagree of Agree | Agree | Strongly Agree |

10. I have created a plan for my development in this line of work/career field.

| Strongly Disagree | Disagree | Neither Disagree of Agree | Agree | Strongly Agree |

11. I do not identify specific goals for my development in this line of work/career field.

| Strongly Disagree | Disagree | Neither Disagree of Agree | Agree | Strongly Agree |

12. I do not often think about my personal development in this line of work/career field.

| Strongly Disagree | Disagree | Neither Disagree of Agree | Agree | Strongly Agree |

The CCM is a 12 question survey that involve day-to-day attitudes towards one's work, their career resilience, and where they see themselves in their work. The subject is asked to rate his or her level of agreement (Strongly Agree, Disagree, Neither Disagree or Agree, Agree, Strongly Agree), although there is no numerical scoring system.

Target Audience: Those interested in career resilience and career identity (employers, employees).

Psychometrics:

Reliability – Examination of the resulting factor structure and item content suggested that there would be little change in domain sampling adequacy or internal consistency reliability if the factors were reduced. Coefficient alpha reliabilities for the three factors were all .81 or above.

Validity – Correcting for attenuation in both measures yields an expected correlation of .75. This marked correspondence between the two measures suggests convergent validity. Two measures, CCM and Blau's Career Commitment Measure.

APPENDIX H: DEMOGRAPHIC QUESTIONNAIRE

What is your gender?

- Male
- Female
- Transgender or gender variant In what year were you born?

In what year were you born?

| -Select- |

Would you describe yourself as:

- American Indian / Native American
- Asian
- Black / African American
- Hispanic / Latino
- White / Caucasian
- Pacific Islander
- Other (please specify)

| |

What is the highest level of education you completed?

- Elementary school only
- Some high school, but did not finish
- Completed high school
- Some college, but did not finish
- Two-year college degree / A.A / A.S.
- Four-year college degree / B.A. / B.S.
- Some graduate work

- Completed Masters or professional degree
- Advanced Graduate work or Ph.D.

How would you describe your current employment status?

- Employed full time
- Employed part time
- Military/Active Duty
- Unemployed

[If participants do not select "unemployed," they will be asked the following:]

How many total years have you been employed? If less than 1 year, please indicate a decimal. For example: 6 months = 0.5 years.

Years	Months
--Select--	--Select--

How many years have you been employed by your current employer?

Years	Months
--Select--	--Select--

Thank You!

APPENDIX I: IRB APPROVAL LETTER

Institutional Review Board - IRB
5757 Plaza Dr., Suite 100 Cypress, California 90630
Tel: (714) 816-0366 • Fax: (714) 226-9844

Date: 3/22/2016

Dear Crystal Washington,

Thank you for submitting your application to the Institutional Review Board. We reviewed your application for your proposed study, 'Do Job-Specific Problems and Individual Problem-Solving Abilities Mediate the Relationships Between Personality and Career Commitment?' Per federal guidelines, we have determined that your study is exempt from further IRB review for the following reason(s):

Research involves only the use of survey procedures in an adult population, and the information is not recorded in a manner that human subjects can be identified (45 CFR 46.101(b)(2))

This approval is valid for one year from the date of this notice. The research must be conducted according to the proposal submitted to the Trident IRB. In order to preserve the anonymity of participants, data may not be reported without a minimum of ten subjects in a subgroup. If changes to the approved protocol need to be made, a revised protocol must be submitted both to your Dissertation Chair and IRB for review and approval.

Sincerely,

Heidi Sato, Ph.D., MPH
Chair - Institutional Review Board (IRB) Director of Institutional Research

GLOSSARY

A.A	Associate of Art
A.S.	Associate of Science
AUT	Alternative Uses Test
B.A.	Bachelor of Arts
B.S.	Bachelor of Science
BFI	Big Five Inventory
CC	Career Commitment
CCM	Career Commitment Measure
CSE	Career Self-Efficacy
CB	Covariance-Based
CB-SEM	Covariance-Based Structural Equation Model
DMIDI	Decision Making Individual Differences Inventory
FFM	Five Factor Model
GSE	General Self-Efficacy
MV	Mediating or Moderating Variable
NEO-PI	Neuroticism-Extraversion-Openness Personality Inventory
OB	Organizational Behavior
OCEAN	Openness to Experience, Conscientiousness, Extraversion, Agreeableness, and Neuroticism
PhD	Doctor of Philosophy
PLS-SEM	Partial Least Squares – Structural Equation Model
PoPES	Perception of the Problem Environment
RAT	Remote Associations Test
RQ	Research Question
SEM	Structural Equation Modeling
TRA	Theory of Reasoned Action

BIBLIOGRAPHY

Aaker, D.A., Kumar, V., & Day, G. S. (2001). *Marketing research (7th ed.)*. New York, NY: John Wiley & Sons.

Ajzen, I. (1988). Attitudes, personality, and behavior. Chicago: Dorsey Press.

Ajzen, I. & Fishbein, M. (1980). *Understanding attitudes and predicting social behavior.*

Englewood Cliffs, NJ: Prentice-Hall.

Ajzen, I., & Fishbein, M. (1975). Belief, attitude, intention and behavior: an introduction to theory and research. Reading, MA: Addison-Wesley.

Allen, M.J., & Yen, W. M. (2002). *Introduction to measurement theory*. Long Grove, IL: Waveland Press.

Allport, G.W. (1961). *Pattern and growth in personality*. New York, NY: Holt, Rinehart &.

Winston. *American Psychiatric Association*.

Aluja, A. & Garcia, L. (2004). Relationships between big five personality factors and values.

Social Behavior and Personality, 32(7), 619-626.

Anderson, S. L., & Betz, N. E. (2001). Sources of social self-efficacy expectations: their measurement and relation to career development. *Journal of Vocational Behavior, 58*, 98–117.

Andi, H. K. (2012). Emotional intelligence and personality traits: a correlational study of MYEIT and BFI. *International Journal of Academic Research in Business and Social Sciences, 2*(10).

Anusic, I., Schimmack, U., Pinkus, R., Lockwood, P. (2009). The nature and structure of correlations among big five ratings: the halo-alpha-beta model. *Journal of Personality and Social Psychology, 97*(6), 1142-1156.

Appelt, K., Milch, K., Handgraaf, M., & Weber, E. (2011). The decision making individual differences inventory and guidelines for the study of individual differences in judgment and decision-making research, *Judgment and Decision Making, 6*(3), 252-262.

Artino, A. R., La Rochelle, J. S., & Durning, S. J. (2010). Second-year medical students' motivational beliefs, emotions, and achievement. *Medical Education, 44*, 203–1212. DOI: 10.1111/j.1365-2923.2010.03712.x.

Aschengrau, A and Seage, G.R (2009). Essential of epidemiology in public health. Sudbury, MA: Jones and Bartlett Baltimore, Maryland.

Ashton-James, C., Maddux, W., Galinsky, A., & Chartrand, T.L. (2009). Who I am depends on how I feel: The role of affect in the expression of culture. *Psychological Science, 20*, 340-346.

Awang, Z. (2012). A Handbook on Structural Equation Modelling Using Amos Graphic (4th ed.). Center for Graduate Studies (CGS). Universiti Teknologi Mara, Kota Bahru Campus.

Bakker, A., Van der Zee, K., Lewig, K., & Dollard, M. (2002). The relationship between the big five personality factors and burnout: a study among volunteer counselors. *The Journal of Social Psychology, 135*, 1-20.

Balthazard, P., Potter, R., & Warren, J. (2002). *The effects of extraversion and expertise on virtual team interaction and performance.* Proceedings of the 35th Hawaii International Conference on System Sciences. Retrieved on December 18, 2014, from: http://www.hicss.hawaii.edu/HICSS_35/HICSSpapers/PDFdocuments/OSVWE01.pdf.

Bandura, A. (1997). *Self-efficacy: The exercise of control.* New York: Freeman.

Barlett, C., & Anderson, C. (2012). Direct and indirect relations between the big 5 personality traits and aggressive and violent behavior. *Personality and Individual Differences, 52*, 870-875.

Baron, R. M., & Kenny, D. A. (1986). The moderator-mediator variable distinction in social psychological research: Conceptual, strategic, and statistical considerations. *Journal of Personality and Social Psychology, 51,* 1173-1182.

Barrick, M. R., & Mount, M. K. (2005). Yes, personality matters: Moving on to more important matters. *Human Performance, 18*, 359-372.

Barrick, M. R., Mount, M. K., & Judge, T. A. (2001). Personality and performance at the beginning of the new millennium: What do we know and where do we go next?

International Journal of Selection and Assessment, 9, 9–30.

Batey M., Chamorro-Premuzic T., Furnham A. (2010). Individual differences in ideational behavior: Can the big five and psychometric intelligence predict creativity scores? *Creativity Research Journal, 22*:90–97.

Bately, M., & Furnham, A. (2008). The relationship between measures of creativity and schizotypy. *Journal of Personality and Individual Differences*, *45*, 816–821.

Beghetto, R. A. (2006). Creative self-efficacy: Correlates in middle and secondary students.

Creativity Research Journal, 18, 447–457.

Bethlehem, J. (2010). Selection bias in web surveys. *International Statistical Review, 78*: 161–188. DOI: 10.1111/j.1751-5823.2010.00112.x.

Blau, G. J. (1985). The measurement and prediction of career commitment. *Journal of Occupational Psychology, 58*: 277–288. DOI: 10.1111/j.2044-8325.1985.tb00201.x.

Blau, G. J. (1988). Further exploring the meaning and measurement of career. Journal of

Vocational Behavior, 32(3), 284-197. DOI: 10.1016/0001-8791(88)90020-6.

Bligh, M., Kohles, J., Pillai, R. (2011). Romancing leadership: past, present, and future. *The Leadership Quarterly*, *22*, 1058-1077.

Bodea, C.N., & Buchman, R. (2012). Competency management system for IT project oriented organizations. *Studies in Computational Intelligence, 402*, 321-324.

Bureau of Labor Statistics. (2015). Monthly Labor Review. Retrieved on October 22, 2015, from: http://www.bls.gov/opub/mlr/2015/home.htm.

Carson, J. (2007). A problem with problem solving: Teaching thinking without teaching knowledge. *The Mathematics Educator, 17*, 7-14.

Carson, K. D., & Bedeian, A. G. (1994). Career commitment: Construction of a measure and examination of its psychometric properties. *Journal of Vocational Behavior, 44*, 237- 262.

Cervone, D., & Peake, P. K. (1986). Anchoring, efficacy, and action: The influence of judgmental heuristics on self-efficacy judgments and behavior. *Journal of Personality and Social Psychology, 50, 492–501.*

Chamorro-Premuzic, T., & Reichenbacher, L. (2008). Effects of personality and threat of evaluation on divergent and convergent thinking. *Journal of Research in Personality, 42,* 1095-1101.

Chang, E. (1999). Career commitment as a complex moderator of organisational commitment and turnover intention. *Human Relations, 52,* 1257–1277.

CheckMarket. (2015). Sample size calculator. Retrieved online: June 2, 2014, from: https://www.checkmarket.com/market-research-resources/sample-size-calculator/.

Chen, G., Gully, S., & Eden, D. (2001). Validation of a new general self-efficacy scale. Organizational Research Methods, 4(1), 62-83.

Chin, W. W. (1998). The partial least squares approach for structural equation modeling. In G. A. Marcoulides (Ed.), Modern methods for business research (pp. 295–236). London: Lawrence Erlbaum Associates.

Chin, W. W., Newsted, P. R. (1999). Structural equation modeling analysis with small samples using partial least squares. In Hoyle, R. H. (Ed.), Statistical strategies for small sample research. Sage, Thousand Oaks.

Choi, J. N. (2004). Individual and contextual predictors of creative performance: The mediating role of psychological processes. *Creativity Research Journal, 16*, 187–199.

Christakos, G., & SpringerLink (Online service). (2011). *Integrative problem-solving in a time of decadence.* Dordrecht; New York: Springer.

Cloninger, C. R., Svrakic, D. M., Przybeck, T. R. (1993). A psychobiological model of temperament and character. *Archives of General Psychiatry,* 50 (12): 975–90. DOI: 10.1001/archpsyc.1993.01820240059008.

Cohen, J. (1988). Statistical power analysis for the behavioral sciences (2nd ed.). Hillsdale, NJ: Lawrence Erlbaum.

Cohen, J., Cohen P., West, S.G., & Aiken, L.S. (2003). *Applied multiple regression/correlation analysis for the behavioral sciences.* Hillsdale, NJ: Lawrence Erlbaum Associates.

Collier, D., Sekhon, J.S., &. Stark, P. (2010). *Statistical models and causal inference, a dialogue with the social sciences.* Cambridge: Cambridge University Press.

Colzato, L., Szapora, A., Lippelt, D., & Hommel, B. (n.d.). Prior meditation practice modulates performance and strategy use in convergent- and divergent -thinking problems. Institute for Psychological Research & Leiden Institute for Brain and

Cognition, Leiden University, Leiden, The Netherlands.

Costa, P. T., Jr., & McCrae, R. R. (1985). *The NEO Personality Inventory manual.* Odessa, FL: Psychological Assessment Resources.

Costa, P. T., Jr., & McCrae, R. R. (1992). *Revised NEO Personality Inventory (NEO-PI-R) and NEO Five-Factor Inventory (NEO-FFI) Professional Manual.* Odessa, FL: Psychological Assessment Resources.

Crane, T. (2003). *The mechanical mind: a philosophical introduction to minds, machines, and mental representation.* New York, NY: Routledge.

Creswell, J.W. (2009). *Research design: Qualitative, quantitative, and mixed methods (3rd ed.).* Thousand Oaks, CA: Sage.

Cropley, A. (2006). In praise of convergent thinking. *Creativity Research Journal, 18*, 391- 404.

Dattalo, P. (2013). Analysis of Multiple Dependent Variables. New York: Oxford University Press.

De Fruyt, F., McCrae, R. R., Szirmák, Z., & Nagy, J. (2004). The five-factor personality inventory as a measure of the five-factor model: Belgian, American, and Hungarian comparisons with the NEO-PI-R. *Assessment, 11*(3): 207–215. DOI: 10.1177/1073191104265800.

De Jong, R. D., Van der Velde, M. E. G. & Jansen, P. G. W. (2001). Openness to experience and growth need strength as moderators between job characteristics and satisfaction. *International Journal of Selection and Assessment, 9*(4), 350-356.

De Young, C. G. (2006). Higher-order factors of the Big Five in a multi-informant sample. *Journal of Personality and Social Psychology, 91,* 1138–1151.

Digman, J. M. (1997). Higher-order factors of the big five. *Journal of Personality and Social Psychology, 73,* 1246–1256.

Edmunds, G.W. (2011). Personality and the healthy lifestyle as predictors of physical health. Can the healthy lifestyle be explained by personality? PhD Dissertation. University of Illinois. Available at: https://www.ideals.illinois.edu/bitstream/handle/2142/24269/Edmonds_Grant.pdf?sequence=1.

Edwards, J. R., & Lambert L. S. (2007). Methods for integrating moderation and mediation: A general analytical framework using moderated path analysis. Psychological Methods, 12, 1-22.

Englert, J. (2008). Understanding personality in multiple sclerosis using a five factor model approach. State University of New York at Buffalo. Counseling, School and Educational Psychology.

Erdle, S., Irwing, P., Rushton, P., & Park, J. (2010). The General Factor of Personality and its relation to self-esteem in 628, 640 Internet respondents. Personality and Individual Differences, 48, 343-346.

Fabrigar, L. R., Wegener, D. T., MacCallum, R. C., & Strahan, E. J. (1999). Evaluating the use of exploratory factor analysis in psychological research. *Psychological Methods*, *4*, 272-299.

Farah, M.J., Haim, C., Sankoorikal, G., & Chatterjee, A. (2009). When we enhance cognition with Adderall, do we sacrifice creativity? A preliminary study. *Psychopharmacology, 202* (1-3): 541-547.

Feehan, P. F., & Johnston, J. A. (1999). The self-directed search and career self-efficacy.

Journal of Career Assessment, 7 (2), 145-159.

Field, A.P. (2009). *Discovering statistics using SPSS*. (3rd ed.). London: Sage.

Fishbein, M., & Ajzen, I. (1980). *Belief, attitude, intention, and behavior: An introduction to theory and research.* Reading, MA: Addison-Wesley.

Fornell, C., & Larcker, D. F. (1981). Evaluating structural equation models with unobservable variables and measurement error. Journal of Marketing Research, 18, 39–50.

Gboyega, A., & Popoola, S. O. (2010). Job satisfaction and career commitment of librarians in federal university libraries in Nigeria, *Library Review, 59* (3), 175 – 184.

George, J. M., & Zhou, J. (2001). When openness to experience and conscientiousness are related to creative behavior: An interactional approach. *Journal of Applied Psychology, 86*, 513-524.

Gidron, D., Koehler, D., & Tversky, A. (1993). Implicit quantification of personality traits.

Personality and Social Psychology Bulletin, 19(5), 594-604.

Goldberg, L. R. (1993). The structure of phenotypic personality traits. *American Psychologist, 48,* 26–34.

Gomez-Mejia, L. R., Balkin, D. B., & Cardy, R. L. (2007). *Managing human resources* (5th ed.). Upper Saddle River, NJ: Pearson Education International.

Gorsuch, R. L. (1983). Factor Analysis (2nd ed.). Hillsdale, NJ: Erbaum.

Goswani, S., Mathew, M., & Chadha, N.K. (2007). Differences in occupational commitment amongst scientists in Indian defence, academic, and commercial R&D organizations. *Vikalpa, 32*, 13-27.

Goulet, L.R., & Singh, P. (2002). Career commitment: A reexamination and an extension. *Journal of Vocational Behavior, 61*, 73-91.

Grady, T. L. (1989). Determinants of career commitment and turnover behavior. *Journal of Vocational Educational Research, 14*(2), 1-21.

Griffin, B., & Hesketh, B. (2004). Why openness to experience is not a good predictor of job performance. International Journal of *Selection and Assessment, 12*, 243-251.

Guilford, J.P. (1967). The nature of human intelligence. New York: McGraw-Hill.

Guilford, J. P., Christensen, P. R., Merrifield, P. R., & Wilson, R. C. (1978). *Alternate uses: Manual of instructions and interpretations*. Orange, CA: Sheridan Psychological Services.

Guilford, J.P. (1983). *The nature of human intelligence*. New York: McGraw-Hill.

Gurven, M., C. von Rueden, M. Massenkoff, H. Kaplan, & M. Vie, L. (2013). How universal is the big five? Testing the five-factor model of personality variation among forager- farmers in the Bolivian Amazon. *Journal of Personality and Social Psychology, 104*, 354-370.

Hackney, C. W. (2012). Personality, Organizational Commitment, and job search behavior: a field study. PhD Dissertation, University of Tennessee. http://trace.tennessee.edu/utk_graddiss/1300.

Hair, J. F., Anderson, R. E., Babin, B. J., Tatman, R. L., & Black, W. C. (2010). *Multivariate data analysis*. Upper Saddle River, NJ: Prentice Hall.

Hair, J. F., Ringle, C. M., & Sarstedt, M. (2011). PLS-SEM: Indeed a silver bullet. *Journal of Marketing Theory and Practice, 19*, 139-151.

Ho, H. C. Y. & Yeung, D. Y. (2015). Effects of occupational future time perspective on managing stressful work situations. *International Journal of Psychology*. DOI: 10.1002/ijop.12144.

Hogan, J., & Holland, B. (2003). Using theory to evaluate personality and job-performance relations: A socioanalytic perspective. *Journal of Applied Psychology, 88*: 100-112.

Holtgreaves, T. (2004). Social desirability and self-reports: Testing models of socially desirable responding. *Personality and Social Psychology Bulletin, 30*, 161-17.

Hu, L., & Bentler, P. M. (1999). Cutoff criteria for fit indexes in covariance structure analysis: Conventional criteria versus new alternatives. *Structural Equation Modeling, 6*, 1-55.

Huey, S., & Weisz, J. (1997). Ego control, ego resiliency, and the five-factor model as predictors of behavioral and emotional problems in clinic-referred children and adolescents. *Journal of Abnormal Psychology, 106*(3), 404-415.

Hunter, L. (2012). Challenging the reported disadvantages of e-questionnaires and addressing methodological issues of online data collection. *Nurse Researcher, 20*, 11-20.

Hunter, J. E., & Schmidt, F. L. (2004). *Methods of meta-analysis: Correcting error and bias in research findings (2nd edition).* Newbury Park, CA: Sage. Hillsdale, NJ.

Imam, S. S., Rahman, R. B. A., Julita, S. Hafiz, S. (2011). General self efficacy, life satisfaction, and type a behavior among university staff. The Fifth Inter PG Research Colloquium: Research in Malaysia and Thailand.

Irving, P.G., Coleman, D.F., & Cooper, C.L. (1997). Further assessment of a three component model of occupational commitment: Generalizability and differences across occupations. *Journal of Applied Psychology 82*, 444-452.

Jannoo, Z., Yap, B., Auchoybur, N., Lazim, M. (2014). 'The Effect of Non-Normality on CB- SEM and PLS-SEM Path Estimates'. World Academy of Science, Engineering and Technology, International Science Index, Mathematical and Computational Sciences, 1(2), 17.

Jaussi, K. B., Randel, A. E., & Dionne, S. D. (2007). I am, I think, and I do: the role of personal identity, self-efficacy, and cross-applications of experiences in creativity at work. *Creativity Research Journal, 19*, 247—258.

John, O. P., & Srivastava, S. (1999). The big-five trait taxonomy: History, measurement, and theoretical perspectives. In L. A. Pervin & O. P. John (Eds.), *Handbook of personality: Theory and Research, 2*, 102–138, New York: Guilford Press.

John, O. P., Donahue, E. M., & Kentle, R. L. (1991). The big five inventory--Versions 4a and 54. Berkeley, CA: University of California, Berkeley, Institute of Personality and Social Research.

John, O. P., Naumann, L. P., & Soto, C. J. (2008). Paradigm shift to the integrative big five trait taxonomy: History, measurement, and conceptual issues. In O. P. John, R. W. Robins, & L. A. Pervin (Eds.), Handbook of personality: Theory and research (pp. 114- 158). New York, NY: Guilford Press.

Jones, T., Caulfield, L., Wilkinson, D., & Weller, L. (2011). The relationship between nonclinical schizotypy and handedness on divergent and convergent creative problem solving tasks. *Creativity Research Journal, 23*, 222-228.

Judge, T.A., Heller, D. & Mount, M.K. (2002). Five factor model of personality and job satisfaction: a meta-analysis. *Journal of Applied Psychology, 87*:530-541.

Judge, T. A., Higgins, C. A, Thorescn, J. C., & Barrick R. M. (1999). The big five personality traits, general mental ability, and career success across the life span. *Personnel Psychology, 52*: 621-652.

Judge, T. A., Klinger, R., Simon, L. S., & Yang, I. (2008). The contribution of personality to organizational behavior and psychology: Findings, criticism, and future research directions. *Social and Personality Psychology Compass*, 1982-2000.

Kaplan, R.M., & Saccuzzo, D.P. (2010). *Psychological testing*. Singapore: Cengage Learning.

Kaplowitz, M.D., M.D., Hadlock, T.D., & Levine, R. (2004). A comparison of web and mail response rates. *Public Opinion Quarterly, 68*, 94-101.

Karwowski, M., Lebuda, I., & Wiśniewska, E. (2012). Measurement of creative self-efficacy and creative role-identity. *High Ability Studies*, 2. Retrieved on December 18, 2014, from: http://maciej1.home.pl/kreator/data/documents/6.pdf.

Kharkhurin, A. (2012). Multilingualism and creativity. Bilingual Education and Bilingualism: 88. MPG Books Group: Great Britain.

Kim, S. W., & Mueller, C. W. (2010). Occupational and organizational commitment in different occupational contexts: The case of South Korea. *Work and Occupations, 28*(3): 3-36.

King, L., Walker, L., & Broyles, S. (1996). Creativity and the five-factor model. *Journal of Research in Personality 30*, 189–203.

Klang, A. (2012). The relationship between personality and job performance in sales: A replication of past research and extension to Swedish context. Stockholm University Department of Psychology.

Klein, H. J., & Lee, S. (2006). The effects of personality on learning: the mediating role of goal setting. *Human Performance, 19*, 43-66.

Kline, R. B. (2010). *Principles and practice of structural equation modeling* (3rd ed.). New York: Guilford Press.

Kline, R. B. (2011). Principles and practice of structural equation modeling (3rd ed.). New York: Guilford.

Knoblauch, D., & Woolfolk Hoy, A. (2008). Maybe I can teach those kids. The influence of contextual factors on student teachers' efficacy beliefs. *Teaching and Teacher Education, 24*, 166-179.

Kwon, O. N., Park, J. S., Park, J. H. (2006). Cultivating divergent thinking in mathematics through an open-ended approach. Asia Pacific Education Review, 7(1), 51-61.

Kuhn, J.T., & Holling, H. (2009). Exploring the nature of divergent thinking: A multilevel analysis. *Thinking Skills and Creativity, 4*, 116-123.

Kuhn, T.S. (2012). *The structure of scientific revolutions* (50th anniversary edition). Chicago, IL: University of Chicago Press.

Kumar, K., & Bakhshi, A. (2010). The five factor model of personality and organizational commitment: Is there a relationship? *Humanity and Social Sciences Journal, 5*, 25-34.

LaHuis, D.M., Martin, N.R., & Avis, J.M. (2005). Investigating non-linear conscientiousness-job performance relations for clerical employees. *Human Performance, 18*, 199-212.

Latham G. P. & Locke, E. A. (2007). New developments in and directions for goal-setting research. *European Psychologist, 12*, 290-300.

Le, H., Oh, I., Robbins, S.B., Ilies, R., Holland, E., & Westrick, P. (2011). Too much of a good thing: Curvilinear relationships between personality traits and job performance. *Journal of Applied Psychology, 96*, 113-133.

Lee, Y. (2004). Student perceptions of problems' structuredness, complexity, situatedness, and information richness and their effects on problem solving performance. Florida State University.

LePine, J. A., Colquitt, J. A., & Erez, A. (2000). Adaptability to changing task contexts: Effects of general cognitive ability, conscientiousness, and openness to experience. *Personnel Psychology*, 53, 563–593.

Lim, H. S., & Choi, J. N. (2009). Testing an alternative relationship between individual and contextual predictors of creative performance. *Social Behavior and Personality, 37*, 117-136.

Locke, E. A., & Latham, G.P. (2006). New directions in goal-setting theory. *Current Directions in Psychological Science, 15*, 265-268.

London, M (1983). Towards a theory of career motivation. *The Academy of Management Review, 8*, 620-623.

Malik, A. (2013). Efficacy, hope, optimism and resilience at workplace – positive organizational behavior. *International Journal of Scientific and Research Publications, 3*(10), 1-4.

Marone, M., & Blauth, C. (2004). *Creating a problem solving culture: Exploring problem resolution in the workplace*. Tampa, FL: Achieve Global Inc.

Martocchio, J. J., & Judge, T. A. (1997). Relationship between conscientiousness and learning in employee training: Mediating influences of self-deception and self-efficacy. *Journal of Applied Psychology, 82*, 764–773.

Marziano, R.J., & Heflebower, R.J. (2011). *Teaching & assessing 21st century skills*. Bloomington, IN: Marzano Research Laboratory.

Matthews, G., Deary, I., & Whiteman, M. (2003). *Personality traits*. Cambridge University Press (2nd ed., pp. 1-33).

Maxwell, S.E. (2004). The persistence of underpowered studies in psychological research: Causes, consequences, and remedies, *Psychological Methods, 9,* 147 - 163.

Mayfield, J., & Mayfield, M. (2012). The relationship between leader motivating language and self-efficacy. A partial least squares model analysis. *Journal of Business Communication, 49,* 357-376.

McAdams, D. P., & Pals, J. L. (2006). A new big five: Fundamental principles for an integrative science of personality. *American Psychologist,* 204-217.

McCrae, R (1987). Creativity, divergent thinking and openness to experience. *Journal of Personality and Social Psychology, 52*, 1258–1265.

McCrae, R. (2010). The place of the FFM in personality psychology. *Psychological Inquiry, 21*, 57-64.

McCrae, R. R., & Costa, P. T., Jr. (2008). The five-factor theory of personality. In O. P. John, R. W. Robins, & L. A. Pervin (Eds.), *Handbook of personality: Theory and research* (3rd ed., pp. 159–181). New York: Guilford.

McCrae, R. R., & John, O. P. (1992). Introduction to the five-factor model and its applications. *Journal of Personality, 60,* 175-215.

McCrae, R. R., Arenberg, D., & Costa, P. T. (1987). Declines in divergent thinking with age: cross-sectional, longitudinal, and cross-sequential analyses. *Psychology and Aging, 2,* 130.

McDonald, J.H. 2014. Handbook of Biological Statistics (3rd ed.). Sparky House Publishing. Mednick, S. A., & Mednick, M. T. (1967). *Examiner's manual, Remote Associates Test.* Boston: Houghton Mifflin.

Mele, Pels, J., & Polese, F. (2010). A brief review of systems theories and their managerial applications. *Service Science 2*(1-2):126-135. http://dx.doi.org/10.1287/serv.2.1_2.126.

Merhar, C. (2013). Small business employee benefits and HR blog. Retrieved on October 23, 2015, from: http://www.zanebenefits.com/blog/bid/312123/Employee-Retention-The-Real-Cost-of-Losing-an-Employee.

Mischel, W. (1971). *Introduction to personality.* New York: Holt, Rinehart & Winston.

Monecke A. & Leisch F. (2012). PLS: Structural equation modeling using partial least squares. *Journal of Statistical Software, 48*(3), 1–32. URL http://www.jstatsoft.org/ v48/i03/.

Mount, M. K., Oh, I., & Burns, M. (2008). Incremental validity of perceptual speed and accuracy over general mental ability. *Personnel Psychology, 61*, 113–139.

Mrayyan, M. T., & Al-Faouri, I. (2008)[1]. Predictors of career commitment and job performance of Jordanian nurses. *Journal of Nursing Management, 16*, 246–256. Mrayyan, M. T. and Al-Faouri, I. (2008)[2], Career Commitment and Job Performance of Jordanian Nurses. Nursing Forum, 43: 24–37. DOI: 10.1111/j.1744-6198.2008.00092.x.

Musek, J. (2007). A general factor of personality: Evidence for the big one in the five-factor model. *Journal of Research in Personality, 41*, 1213–1233.

Niles, S. G., & Sowa, C. J. (1992). Mapping the nomological network of career self-efficacy. *The Career Development Quarterly, 41*, 13–21. DOI: 10.1002/j.2161- 0045.1992.tb00351.x.

Nunnally, J. C., & Bernstein, I. H. (1994). Psychometric theory (3rd ed.). New York: McGraw-Hill.

O'Connor, B.P. (2002). A quantitative review of the comprehensiveness of the five-factor model in relation to popular personality inventories. *Assessment*, 9, 188-203.

Paulhus, D.L. (1991) Measurement and control of response bias. In J. P. Robinson, P. R. Shaver, & L. S. Wrightsman (Eds.). *Measures of personality and social psychological attitudes*, 1(2), 17-60. San Diego, CA: Academic Press.

Paulhus, D. L., & John, O. P. (1998). Egoistic and moralistic biases in self-perception: The interplay of self-deceptive styles with basic traits and motives. *Journal of Personality, 66*, 1025–1060.

Pearl, J. (2009). Causal inference in statistics: an overview. *Statistics Surveys, 4*, 96-146.

Persson, S. (2009). *The interaction effect of effortful control and neuroticism on problem solving.* Institutionen for Psykologi, Lunds Universitet.

Pierce, J.R., & Aguinis, H. (2013). The too-much-of-a-good-thing effect in management. *Journal of Management, 39*, 313-338.

Podsakoff, P.M., Bommer, W.H., Podsakoff, N.P., & MacKenzie, S.B. (2006). Relationships between leader reward and punishment behavior and subordinate attitudes, perceptions, and behaviors: A meta-analytic review of existing and new research. *Organizational Behavior and Human Decision Processes, 99*, 113-142.

Poon, J.M.L. (2004). Career commitment and career success: moderating role of emotion perception. *Career Development International, 9,* 374-390.

Prat-Sala, M., & Redford, P. (2010). The interplay between motivation, self-efficacy, and approaches to studying. *British Journal of Educational Psychology, 80* (2), 283-305.

PsychData. (2016). Create online surveys with confidence and ease. Retrieved on February 25, 2016: https://www.psychdata.com/.

Rammstedt, B., & John, O. P. (2007). Measuring personality in one minute or less: A 10-item short version of the big five inventory in English and German. *Journal of Research in Personality, 41,* 203–212.

Rashid, H. & Zhao, L. The significance of career commitment in generating commitment to organizational change among information technology personnel. *Academy of Information and Management Sciences Journal.* Retrieved on Oct 21 2015, from: http://www.thefreelibrary.com/The+significance+of+career+commitment+in+generating+commitment+to...-a0241861855.

Ravasi, D., & Schultz, M. (2006). Responding to organizational identity threats: exploring the role of organizational culture. *Academy of Management Journal, 49*, 433–458.

Ray, W.J. (2006). *Methods towards a science of behaviour and experience* (8th ed.). Belmont, CA: Wadsworth.

Reinartz, W. J., Haenlein, M., & Henseler, J. (2009). An empirical comparison of the efficacy of covariance-based and variance-based SEM. International Journal of Research in Marketing 26, 332–344.

Riveros, A.M.M., & Tsai T, S-T., (2011). Career commitment and organizational commitment in for-profit and non-profit sectors. *International Journal of Emerging Sciences, 1*, 324-30.

Rushton, J. P., & Irwing, P. (2008). A general factor of personality from two meta-analyses of the big five: Digman (1997) and Mount, Barrick, Scullen, and Rounds (2005).

Sarstedt, M., Ringle, C. M., Henseler, J., & Hair, J. F. (2014). On the emancipation of PLS- SEM. Long Range Planning, 47, 154–160.

Sawatzky, R.G., Ratner, P.A., Richardson, C.G., Washburn, C., Sudmant, W., & Mirwaldt, P. (2012) Stress and depression in students: The mediating role of stress management self- efficacy. *Nursing Research, 61*, 13-21. http://dx.doi.org/10.1097/NNR.0b013e31823b1440.

Schneider, B. (2007). Evolution of the study and practice of personality at work. *Human Resources Management, 46*, 583–610. DOI: 10.1002/hrm.20183.

Schwarzer, R., & Jerusalem, M. (1995). Generalized self-efficacy scale. In J. Weinman, S. Wright, & M. Johnston, Measures in health psychology: A user's portfolio. Causal and control beliefs (pp. 35-37). Windsor, UK: NFER-NELSON.

Shin, E., Johnson, T.P., & Rao, K. (2012). Survey mode effects on data quality: Comparison of web and mail modes in a U.S. national panel survey. *Social Science Computer Review, 30*, 212-228.

Simola, S. (2011). Relationship between occupational commitment and ascribed importance of organisational characteristics, *Education + Training, 53*(1), 67-81.

Stilson, F. (2005). Master Thesis: "Does agreeableness help a team perform a problem solving task?" University of South Florida, Scholar Commons, Graduate School of Theses and Dissertations.

Tett, R. (1998). *Is conscientiousness always positively related to job performance*? Professional Paper, *Society for Industrial & Organizational Psychology, Inc.* Retrieved on December 18, 2014, from: http://www.siop.org/tip/backissues/TIPJuly98/tett.aspx.

Tierney, P., & Farmer, S. M. (2002). Creative self-efficacy: Potential antecedents and relationship to creative performance. *Academy of Management Journal, 45*, 1137–1148.

Tierney, P., & Farmer, S. M. (2010). Creative self-efficacy development and creative performance over time. *Journal of Applied Psychology, 30*, 413– 432.

Tupes, E.C., & Christal, R.E. (1992). Recurrent personality factors based on trait ratings. *Journal of Personality*, *60* (2), 225-251.

Turel, O., & Zhang, Y. (2010). Does virtual team composition matter? Trait and problem solving configurations effects on team performance. *Behaviour & Information Technology, 29* (4), 363-375.

Vancouver, J. B., & Day, D. V. (2005). Industrial and organisation research on self- regulation: From constructs to applications. *Applied Psychology, 54,* 155–185.

Voss, F., Greene, T.R., Post, T.A., & Penner, B.C. (2004). Problem solving skills in the social sciences. In: K.W. Spence & J.T. Spence (Eds.). *The Psychology of Learning and Motivation, 17.* San Diego, CA: Academic Press.

Wallin, L., Bostrom, A.M., & Gustavsson, J.P. (2012). Capability beliefs regarding evidence- based practice are associated with application of EBP and research use: Validation of a new measure. *Worldviews Evidence Based Nursing, 9,* 139-148.

Wechsung, I. (2014). An Evaluation Framework for Multimodal Interaction: Determining Quality Aspects and Modality Choice. New York: Springer. DOI: 10.1007/978-3-319- 03810-0.

Weiner, I. B., Freedhein, D. K., Schinka, J. A., & W. F. Velicer. (2003). Handbook of Psychology. New York: Wiley.

Werner, P. (2004). Reasoned action and planned behavior. In S. J. Peterson & T. S. Bredow (Eds.), Middle range theories: Application to nursing research (pp. 125-147). Philadelphia, PA: Lippincott, Williams, & Wilkins.

Wetzels, M., Odekerken-Schroder, G., & van Oppen, C. (2009). Using PLS path modeling for assessing hierarchical construct models: Guidelines and empirical illustration, *MIS Quarterly, 33 (1),* 177-195.

Wigert, B. (2012). The influence of divergent and convergent problem construction processes on creative problem solving. PhD Dissertation: University of Nebraska. Retrieved on December 28, 2014, from: http://gradworks.umi.com/36/04/3604561.html.

Wigert, B. (2013). The influence of divergent and convergent problem construction processes on creative problem solving. Retrieved on December 7, 2015, from: http://search.proquest.com/docview/1475225506.

Wiggins, J. S. (ed.). (1996). *The five-factor model of personality: Theoretical perspectives.* New York: Guilford.

Yoon, S. & Horne, C. (2004). Accruing the sample in survey research. *Southern Online Journal of Nursing Research, 5*(2). Retrieved on November 16, 2015, from: http://www.resourcenter.net/images/snrs/files/sojnr_articles/iss02vol05.htm.

Zikmund, W., Babin, B.J., Carr, J.C., & Griffin, M. (2010). Business research methods (8th ed.). Mason, OH: Thomson/South-Western.

Zimmerman, B. J. (2000). Self-efficacy: An essential motive to learn. *Contemporary Educational Psychology, 25*, 82-91.

www.ingramcontent.com/pod-product-compliance
Lightning Source LLC
Chambersburg PA
CBHW051312220526
45468CB00004B/1306